Ashes to Fire

YEAR C

DAILY REFLECTIONS FROM ASH WEDNESDAY TO PENTECOST

EDITED BY
MERRITT J. NIELSON

BEACON HILL PRESS
OF KANSAS CITY

Copyright 2012 by Beacon Hill Press of Kansas City

ISBN 978-0-8341-4163-6

Cover Design: Doug Bennett
Interior Design: Sharon Page

Illustrations by Keith Alexander

Unless otherwise indicated, all Scripture quotations are from the *New Revised Standard Version* (NRSV) of the Bible, copyright 1989 by the Division of Christian Education of the National Council of the Churches of Christ in the USA. Used by permission. All rights reserved.

Permission to quote from the following additional versions of the Bible is acknowledged with appreciation:

The *Holy Bible, New Living Translation* (NLT), copyright 1996, 2004, 2007 by Tyndale House Foundation. Used by permission of Tyndale House Publishers, Inc., Carol Stream, IL 60188. All rights reserved.

Scripture quotations marked KJV are from the King James Version.

Text marked BCP is from the 1979 *Book of Common Prayer* (New York: Church Hymnal Corporation, 1979).

Contents

Gloria — 5
Preface — 6
Lenten Season — 11
  Lenten Season—The Prelude: Who's the Good Guy? — 12
    Ash Wednesday—Saturday — 16
  Lenten Season—Week 1 — 21
    Sunday: A Wilderness Survival Guide — 22
    Monday—Saturday — 26
  Lenten Season—Week 2 — 33
    Sunday: Jerusalem, Jerusalem! — 34
    Monday—Saturday — 38
  Lenten Season—Week 3 — 45
    Sunday: About-Face—Beautiful! — 46
    Monday—Saturday — 50
  Lenten Season—Week 4 — 57
    Sunday: Coming to Our Senses — 58
    Monday—Saturday — 62
  Lenten Season—Week 5 — 69
    Sunday: And the Fragrance Filled the House — 70
    Monday—Saturday — 74
  Lenten Season—Week 6 (Holy Week) — 81
    Palm Sunday: Praise Is God's Alone — 82
    Monday—Wednesday — 88
    Maundy Thursday — 91
    Good Friday — 92
    Holy Saturday — 93

- Easter Season — 95
  - Easter Season—Week 1 — 95
    - Resurrection Sunday: Where Is He? — 96
    - Monday—Saturday — 100
  - Easter Season—Week 2 — 107
    - Sunday: Life's Locked-Door Seasons — 108
    - Monday—Saturday — 114
  - Easter Season—Week 3 — 121
    - Sunday: Hook or Crook? — 122
    - Monday—Saturday — 126
  - Easter Season—Week 4 — 133
    - Sunday: Tell Us Plainly — 134
    - Monday—Saturday — 138
  - Easter Season—Week 5 — 145
    - Sunday: The New Commandment — 146
    - Monday—Saturday — 150
  - Easter Season—Week 6 — 157
    - Sunday: The Promise of God's Peace — 158
    - Monday—Wednesday — 164
    - Ascension Thursday — 167
    - Friday—Saturday — 168
  - Easter Season—Week 7 — 171
    - Ascension Sunday: As Long As It Takes — 172
    - Monday—Saturday — 178
- Pentecost Sunday — 185
  - Pentecost: The Fullness of Life in the Spirit — 186
- *Sources* — 191

GLORIA*

Glory to God in the highest,
and peace to his people on earth.

Lord God, heavenly King,
almighty God and Father,
we worship you, we give you thanks,
we praise you for your glory.

Lord Jesus Christ, only Son of the Father,
Lord God, Lamb of God,
you take away the sin of the world;
have mercy on us;
you are seated at the right hand of the Father;
receive our prayer.

For you alone are the Holy One,
you alone are the Lord,
you alone are the Most High,
Jesus Christ,
with the Holy Spirit,
in the glory of God the Father. Amen.
*BCP

A Journey with Jesus from Ash Wednesday to Pentecost

Ashes to Fire is an intentional journey with Jesus from Ash Wednesday through Holy Week and Easter and on to Pentecost Sunday—*from penitence to praise to power*. Central to the Ashes to Fire experience is this daily devotional guide—the *Ashes to Fire Year C Devotional*—a combination of Scripture reading, prayer, corporate worship, small-group Bible study, and personal journaling.

Using the Scripture readings from Year C of the *Revised Common Lectionary*, a devotional reflection based on the Sunday gospel passage begins each week and serves as the main content for Sunday school and small groups. Daily readings—Monday through Saturday—come from the Old and New Testaments and are accompanied with prayers and spiritual insights from men and women of faith who have helped to form, and continue to shape, our Christian tradition. Graphics and music written specifically for the Ashes to Fire journey provide personal inspiration and spiritual enrichment.

Enhancing this devotional guide are additional resources for worship services and small-group meetings or Sunday school classes. The total Ashes to Fire experience encourages entire congregations—children, youth, and adults—to engage the same passages of Scripture in Christian proclamation, education, and faith formation. This spiritual adventure has already inspired thousands of Christians in hundreds of congregations in a quest for personal and corporate renewal.

Like Christians of earlier eras, we often find ourselves hungering to know God more deeply and intimately. One of the best ways to satisfy that hunger is to immerse ourselves in the Sacred Scriptures. John, in remembering the words of Jesus, gives us a key insight: "You search the scriptures because you *think* that *in them* you have eternal life; and it is they that testify on my behalf"

(John 5:39, emphasis added). When we immerse ourselves in the Written Word, we hear it testify to the Living Word and find ourselves in an ever-deepening relationship with Jesus. In this devotional guide you will discover a breadth and depth of Bible reading, spiritual reflection, and prayer that could, if faithfully followed, inspire the transforming, life-renewing experience with Christ for which your heart hungers.

While you will find the companion resources for the Ashes to Fire experience at www.ashestofire.com and in the Ashes to Fire media kit available from the publisher, remember that this devotional guide is the heart and soul of the journey. Here are the compass points for those who want to join others on this pilgrimage and rehearse with them the stories of our shared faith.

THE LENTEN AND EASTER SEASONS

The season of Lent begins with Ash Wednesday and continues for six weeks. Palm Sunday, the sixth Sunday of Lent, marks the beginning of Holy Week, which includes Maundy Thursday, Good Friday, and Holy Saturday, the day before Easter/Resurrection Sunday. The first Sunday of Easter marks the beginning of the season of Easter, fifty days that lead up to Pentecost Sunday. In total, these fourteen weeks will give shape and substance for reflection, study, and proclamation. During the week, expanded readings in the Gospels will put us in touch with the One to whom they testify—Jesus of Nazareth, the Christ.

Using the Ashes to Fire Devotional and Study Guide

THE LENTEN PRELUDE

Ash Wednesday begins the Lenten season. Our devotional reflection for this first day in our Lenten journey focuses on the contrast between the proud Pharisee and the penitent prayer of the publican in the temple: "God, be merciful to me, a sinner!" (Luke 18:13). Our writer for the day concludes, "Whether we come from a deeply religious life or a fairly pagan life, our hope is Jesus . . . Share in the hopeful cry of people through the ages, 'Jesus, Savior, have mercy on me!' And he does. Thanks be to God!"

The next three days—Thursday, Friday, and Saturday—follow a pattern of personal daily devotions that will be repeated every weekday during the Lenten and Easter seasons, concluding on the Saturday before Pentecost Sunday.

THE MONDAY THROUGH SATURDAY DEVOTIONAL PAGES

Each day of the fourteen-week period follows a similar pattern consisting of Morning Meditations and Evening Reflections. Four Scripture readings are included per day—one from the Old Testament, one from the Psalms, one from the Epistles, and one from the Gospels. If you do not have time to read these passages in their entirety, each of the first three is summarized for you. It is suggested that you always complete the daily gospel lesson in its entirety.

The Bible readings for each day are not necessarily related thematically, although on some days the Scripture selections seem to speak with one voice.* Throughout the weeks you will be reading substantial portions of particular books of the Bible. For instance, during the weeks after Easter all of the New Testament readings follow the history of the early church in the Acts of the Apostles. The gospel readings are all taken from the Upper Room Discourse (John 13—16) and the High Priestly Prayer of Jesus in John 17. The Old Testament readings track with the prophets Isaiah, Zechariah, and Malachi.

We also provide in the daily devotional guides a series of inspirational quotations and reflective prayers from men and women of faith who keep us connected with our shared Christian heritage.

Each evening an excerpt from the Psalms and a brief prayer provide preludes to nighttime rest and renewal. Once again, many of the prayers are adapted extracts from John Wesley's *Forms of Prayer*. Those prayers are identified with a **JW** icon.

THE SUNDAY DEVOTIONAL REFLECTION PAGES

Each Sunday, a devotional reflection based on a key gospel narrative or teaching provides a background resource for Sunday school class conversations or small-group study. The reflection expresses what a particular writer thinks about the passage. The purpose of this devotional approach is to encourage your engagement with and response to the same portion of Scripture.

In addition to reading the gospel narrative and the devotional reflection, you should also read the suggested companion passages, usually one from the Old Testament, one from the Psalms, and one from the New Testament Epistles. Discussion prompts are intended to enhance your experience with the gospel reading and encourage your participation in group discussions.

---

*In Lent, the psalm is most closely related to the Old Testament lesson, while in the Easter season it often connects with the readings from the Acts of the Apostles.

The Reflective Journaling section provides an opportunity for you to record any insights and prayers that arise from the day's study.

THE ART AND MUSIC OF ASHES TO FIRE

Included with this devotional guide are fourteen freshly minted songs for the Ashes to Fire experience. The music is intended for your inspirational reflection, as well as for use in both corporate and small-group worship settings.

Each week, a piece of artwork focuses on the theme of the Sunday gospel reading. This year the art features the creative talents of artist Keith Alexander.

This edition contains all new material—Scripture readings, devotional reflections, prayers, and music—based on Year C of the *Revised Common Lectionary*. Together with its trademark interior graphic design and its leatherette binding, the *Ashes to Fire Year C Devotional* provides a resource that seamlessly integrates the message of the Christian faith and a medium that evokes a sacred reverence for the gospel of Christ into a one-of-a-kind faith-forming experience for the entire church. The ultimate goal is personal spiritual renewal and congregational revival as we set out on our journey and embrace God's loving intention that our "hearts [might be] strangely warmed" (John Wesley) and filled to capacity with the love of God. Perhaps the book you hold in your hands will be the answer to your own soul's longings for a relationship with the Lord that will forever change your life. God be with you, pilgrim. Let's take the journey together.

For the Ashes to Fire Team
Merritt J. Nielson
Curriculum Director

We acknowledge a debt of gratitude to our primary writers for the devotional reflections in this journal: Shane Ash, Jill Bowling, John Bowling, Chris Folmsbee, Helen Metcalfe, Russell F. Metcalfe Jr., Frank Moore, Mary Rearick Paul, Elizabeth Perry, Rick Power, Bud Reedy, Jeren Rowell, and Grant Zweigle. Please visit www.ashestofire.com for other resources, including Sunday school and small-group discussion guides for children, youth, and adults; sermon and worship suggestions; and music for public services.

PLEASE NOTE: **This devotional journal is an undated resource. Consult a church calendar or lectionary for specific dates for use during the current year.**

LENTEN SEASON

Ash Wednesday
Who's the Good Guy?

Read Luke 18:9-14, the introductory reflection titled "Who's the Good Guy?" and then the additional devotional material for Ash Wednesday on page 16.

THE MUSIC OF ASHES TO FIRE

Prelude Days: "Gloria" (Track 1)

Thursday through Saturday

IN THE MORNING:

A personal daily devotional guide includes prayer, a psalm, and readings from the Old Testament, the Epistles, and the Gospels for each day of the week.

In addition to the daily psalms, the Bible readings for the Lenten Prelude come from Jonah, Deuteronomy, Isaiah, Titus, Hebrews, and the gospels of Luke and Matthew.

Inspirational quotes from men and women of faith keep us in contact with our shared Christian heritage.

IN THE EVENING:

An evening psalm and prayer become preludes to nighttime rest and renewal.

ASH WEDNESDAY

LENTEN SEASON—THE PRELUDE
Who's the Good Guy?

A devotional reflection based on Luke 18:9-14

I have a little brother and we had some wonderful times playing together as kids. We were inseparable. They called us "me and my shadow." Wherever I went, Jay was never far behind. Oh, we had our share of disagreements. Usually they were over who was going to be the "good guy" and who had to be the "bad guy." We knew from our weekly watching of *Gunsmoke* that there had to be a good guy and a bad guy. You just couldn't play cowboys effectively in any other way.

We also knew that it was pretty easy to tell which was which. Do you know how? The good guy wore a white hat, and the bad guy wore a black hat. Simple, wasn't it? At least I thought it was simple because I had blond hair and my little brother had dark hair. This obviously (in my mind) made me the good guy and my brother the villain. We did have some fights over this matter, but overall, life was pretty simple back then. As far as we knew, there were basically two kinds of people—good guys and bad guys. We learned that lesson well. We even learned how to apply that lesson to other areas of life and became adept at categorizing people on the basis of a few external signs.

I begin here because of the potential problem in this text from Luke's gospel. It is likely that our first read of this story has us categorizing these men. It's really not difficult. One is a Pharisee, and we know he must be bad because Jesus seemed to criticize Pharisees more than any other group. None of us wants to be *pharisaical*, so clearly the Pharisee is the bad guy.

And the tax collector—well, he's not the greatest guy in the world either. In fact, he's a pretty shady character, but apparently he does something right, because Jesus says he went home justified. The story portrays him as the good guy. So there you have it. Pharisee—bad; humble publican—good. End of lesson.

There is just one problem. This neat categorizing of characters may cause us to miss the key point of Jesus' story. If we're not careful, we could leave this parable saying to ourselves, "God, I thank thee that I am not like the Pharisee." The fact is, the Pharisee here is no villain. He is upright and holy. He goes beyond the requirements of the law. The law said, "Fast twice a year," but he fasted twice a week. We may criticize his prayer, but what's wrong with it? He begins by expressing thanks to God. How often do we launch into our list of needs without giving thanks? Only one thing is really wrong with his prayer: he doesn't seem to realize how badly he still needs God, and he doesn't ask for any of God. As one preacher said, "He asks nothing and gets what he asks for."

On the other hand, Jesus' hearers know that if anyone in all of Judaism should go home from the temple unjustified, it should be a tax collector. He had likely cheated many of them out of hard-earned money. He is not a good man. And his apparent humility is really not presented as something for us to copy; it's just an honest admission of his woefulness. He has nothing to offer, but at least he knows it.

Now so far there's really nothing in this story to shock us. The Pharisee is as we would expect him, and the tax collector is as we would expect him. Good guys and bad guys—we know how this goes. But just about the time Jesus' hearers are getting ready to line up with the good guy, he pulls the rug out from under their feet. Here's the shocker: it's the tax collector who goes home justified, not the Pharisee. How can that be?

We almost automatically think that God must have a special place in his heart for those who "do it right." The truth is, God has a special place in his heart for anyone who will simply acknowledge his or her need. Perhaps this story is not really about either of these two men. Maybe it has nothing to do with who is good and who is bad. Maybe the real point here is something about a God who does not share our neat categories.

The fact is, we are like both of these men. These are the two kinds of people you tend to find in worship—Pharisees and publicans. Some of us are one of them all the time. Most of us are each of them some of the time. There are times when we come to worship as good, Bible-believing, righteous Pharisees who ask nothing of God and get nothing. We are so pleased with ourselves that all we achieve on a Sunday morning is getting our church attendance card punched.

But there are also times we come as publicans, needing everything. We feel lost and nearly without hope. Then grace breaks through, God meets us in worship, and we return home with more than we even dared asked for. Could it be that before this story says anything about us, it means to announce something wonderful about God?

As we begin this Lenten journey, we may have a great temptation to play a role before God. Some of us may be tempted to play the Pharisee, truly thankful for our good life but seeking and finding nothing fresh from God's transforming power in our lives. Others of us may be tempted to play the publican, beating our chests, denying ourselves, and working up a good grief as we remember the passion of our Lord.

The important truth is that neither posture earns the favor of God. Where you come from is not the issue. Your performance during these weeks is not the issue. Whatever categories into which this world or even the church wants to place you in is not the issue. White hat or black hat, good guy or bad guy, is not the issue.

None of us has anything to bring but our true selves. But right there is where good news emerges. There is grace in Jesus. Whether we come from a deeply religious life or a fairly pagan life, our hope is Jesus. Come to Jesus, and share in the hopeful cry of people through the ages, "Jesus, Savior, have mercy on me!" And he does. Thanks be to God! —Jeren Rowell

Reflective Journaling

ASH WEDNESDAY • LENTEN SEASON

ASH WEDNESDAY
DAY 1 — LENTEN SEASON

PSALM 32 ▪ JONAH 3:1—4:11 ▪ HEBREWS 12:1-14 ▪ LUKE 18:9-14

MORNING MEDITATIONS

PRAYER—O God, in my passage through this world, do not let my heart become its slave. But always fix my undivided attention on the prize of my high calling. Let me do this one thing: let me press towards this goal with such zeal that everything I do today will help me reach that goal. Prepare my heart for that pure bliss that you are preparing for all those who love you. Amen. **JW**

PSALM 32:5—Then I acknowledged my sin to you, and I did not hide my iniquity; I said, "I will confess my transgressions to the LORD," and you forgave the guilt of my sin.

JONAH 3:5-8 *Cry Mightily to God*
And the people of Nineveh believed God; they proclaimed a fast, and everyone, great and small, put on sackcloth . . . the king of Nineveh . . . rose from his throne, removed his robe, covered himself with sackcloth, and sat in ashes. Then he had a proclamation made in Nineveh . . . "Cry mightily to God. All shall turn from their evil ways and from the violence that is in their hands."

HEBREWS 12:1b-2a *Lay Aside Every Sin*
Let us also lay aside every weight and the sin that clings so closely, and let us run with perseverance the race that is set before us, looking to Jesus the pioneer and perfecter of our faith.

LUKE 18:9-14 *Today's Gospel Reading*

> May God see our eager desire. May the Lord Jesus Christ look at the purpose of our mind and faith. He will give the larger rewards of his glory to those with a greater desire for him.
> — ST. CYPRIAN, *TREATISE 7*, PARA. 26

EVENING REFLECTIONS

PSALM 102:1-2—Hear my prayer, O LORD; let my cry come to you. Do not hide your face from me in the day of my distress. Incline your ear to me; answer me speedily in the day when I call.

PRAYER—Father, grant me forgiveness of what is past, and a perfect repentance of all my failings that in the days to come I may with a pure spirit, do your will—walking humbly with you, showing love to all, keeping my soul in holiness, and my body in sanctification and honor, in Jesus' name. Amen. **JW**

THURSDAY
DAY 2 — LENTEN SEASON

PSALM 1 • DEUTERONOMY 30:15-20 • TITUS 1:1-16 • LUKE 9:21-25

MORNING MEDITATIONS

PRAYER—Lord God, send your Holy Spirit to be the guide of all my ways and the sanctifier of my soul and body. Give me the light of your presence, your peace from heaven, and the salvation of my soul, through Jesus Christ my Lord. Amen. *JW*

PSALM 1:1-2—Happy are those who do not follow the advice of the wicked, or take the path that sinners tread, or sit in the seat of scoffers; but their delight is in the law of the Lord, and on his law they meditate day and night.

DEUTERONOMY 30:19-20a *Choose Life*
I call heaven and earth to witness against you today that I have set before you life and death, blessings and curses. Choose life so that you and your descendants may live, loving the Lord your God, obeying him and holding fast to him.

TITUS 1:3-4 *Grace and Peace from God*
In due time he revealed his word through the proclamation with which I have been entrusted by the command of God our Savior. To Titus, my loyal child in the faith we share: Grace and peace from God the Father and Christ Jesus our Savior.

LUKE 9:21-25 *Today's Gospel Reading*

> We must be persuaded how much God loved us so that we don't shrink from him in despair. And we need to be shown also what kind of people we are whom he loved so that we also don't withdraw from him out of pride.   ST. AUGUSTINE, *ON THE TRINITY* (4.1)

EVENING REFLECTIONS

PSALM 37:3-5—Trust in the Lord, and do good; so you will live in the land, and enjoy security. Take delight in the Lord, and he will give you the desires of your heart. Commit your way to the Lord; trust in him, and he will act.

PRAYER—My Lord and my God, I turn to you in sincerity of heart and, renouncing all self-interest, give myself up entirely to you. I desire to be yours and only yours forever. O my Savior and Sanctifier, turn your face to this poor soul who seeks you and accept the gift of myself. Amen. *JW*

FRIDAY — DAY 3, LENTEN SEASON

PSALM 51:3-4, 5-6, 18-19 ▪ **ISAIAH 58:1-9a** ▪ **TITUS 2:1-15** ▪ **MATTHEW 9:14-17**

MORNING MEDIATIONS

PRAYER—O God, you instruct me with your laws, you redeem me by the blood of your Son, and you sanctify me by the grace of your Holy Spirit. For these and all other mercies, how can I ever worthily love you or magnify your great and glorious name? Forever, I will bless you and adore your goodness. Amen. *JW*

PSALM 51:4—Against you, you alone, have I sinned, and done what is evil in your sight, so that you are justified in your sentence and blameless when you pass judgment.

ISAIAH 58:6-7a, 8a   *Your Light Shall Break Forth*
Is not this the fast that I choose: to loose the bonds of injustice, to undo the thongs of the yoke, to let the oppressed go free, and to break every yoke? Is it not to share your bread with the hungry . . . Then your light shall break forth like the dawn, and your healing shall spring up quickly.

TITUS 2:11-12   *Live Godly Lives*
For the grace of God has appeared, bringing salvation to all, training us to renounce impiety and worldly passions, and in the present age to live lives that are self-controlled, upright and godly.

MATTHEW 9:14-17   *Today's Gospel Reading*

> If we want to have boldness, we must clear away our anger so that no one can attribute our words to it. No matter how sound your words may be, no matter how boldly you speak, how fairly you correct, you ruin everything when you speak with anger.
>
> — ST. CHRYSOSTOM, *"HOMILY NO. 17" ON ACTS*

EVENING REFLECTIONS

PSALM 35:18, 22, 24ab—I will thank you in the great congregation; in the mighty throng I will praise you . . . You have seen, O Lord; do not be silent! O Lord, do not be far from me . . . Vindicate me, O Lord, my God, according to your righteousness.

PRAYER—O Lord of Life, put your grace into my heart, that I may worthily magnify your great and glorious name. You have made me and sent me into the world to do your work. Assist me to fulfill the purpose of my creation, and to show your praise by giving myself always to your service. *JW*

SATURDAY — DAY 4, LENTEN SEASON

PSALM 86:1-7 • ISAIAH 58:9b-14 • TITUS 3:1-15 • LUKE 5:27-32

MORNING MEDITATIONS

PRAYER—Everlasting God, I bless you with my whole heart and thank you for your goodness to me. Watch over me today with eyes of mercy; strengthen my soul and body according to your will, and fill my heart with your Holy Spirit that I may live this day, and all the rest of my days, to your glory. Amen. **JW**

PSALM 86:4-5—Gladden the soul of your servant, for to you, O Lord, I lift up my soul. For you, O Lord, are good and forgiving, abounding in steadfast love to all who call on you.

ISAIAH 58:13a, 13c, 14a   *You Shall Ride upon the Heights*
If you refrain from trampling the sabbath, from pursuing your own interests on my holy day . . . if you honor it, not going your own ways . . . then you shall take delight in the Lord, and I will make you ride upon the heights of the earth.

TITUS 3:3-5a   *He Saved Us*
For we ourselves were once foolish, disobedient, led astray, slaves to various passions and pleasures, passing our days in malice and envy, despicable, hating one another. But when the goodness and loving kindness of God our Savior appeared, he saved us . . . according to his mercy.

LUKE 5:27-32   *Today's Gospel Reading*

> Let us be prepared for the will of God with a sound mind, a firm faith, and strong virtue. Laying aside the fear of death, let us think on the eternal life to come. Through this knowledge let us demonstrate that we are what we believe.   ST. CYPRIAN, *TREATISE 7*, PARA. 24

EVENING REFLECTIONS

PSALM 43:3-4—O send out your light and your truth; let them lead me; let them bring me to your holy hill and to your dwelling. Then I will go to the altar of God . . . and I will praise you . . . O God, my God.

PRAYER—O God the Father, have mercy upon me. O God the Son, who knowing the Father's will, came into the world to save me, have mercy upon me. O God the Holy Spirit, who for the same purpose sanctified me in baptism and has breathed holy thoughts into me, have mercy upon me. Amen. **JW**

WEEK ONE
Lenten Season

Sunday: A Wilderness Survival Guide

Read the gospel passage from Luke 4:1-13 and the devotional reflection titled "A Wilderness Survival Guide," then respond to the discussion prompts in the Reflective Journaling section.

THE MUSIC OF ASHES TO FIRE

Week 1: "I Need No Other Argument" (Track 2)

Monday through Saturday

IN THE MORNING:

A personal daily devotional guide includes prayer, a reading from the Old Testament, the Psalms, the Epistles, and the Gospels for each day of the week.

In addition to the daily psalm, this week's readings come from Genesis, Leviticus, Isaiah, Amos, Esther, Ezekiel, Deuteronomy, Galatians, and the gospels of Matthew and Luke.

Inspirational quotes from men and women of faith keep us in contact with our shared Christian heritage.

IN THE EVENING:

An evening psalm and prayer become preludes to nighttime rest and renewal.

SUNDAY

LENTEN SEASON—WEEK ONE
A Wilderness Survival Guide

A devotional reflection based on Luke 4:1-13

Read the gospel passage first, then the devotional reflection that follows. The discussion prompts at the end will help prepare you for Sunday school and small-group sessions.

The contrast is dramatic. One moment Jesus is baptized in the Jordan River, with the Holy Spirit descending on him as a dove. The next moment he is led into the wilderness to be tested. From the well-watered valley to the parched desert. From the companionship of friends to the loneliness of solitude. From fullness to emptiness. From strength to weakness. Or so it seems. But as we will see, appearances can be deceiving.

From all we can tell, Jesus made no preparations for this extended survival exercise. He didn't take a backpack, a tent, or even a Swiss Army knife. The Judean desert is not a welcoming place. Like most deserts, it's barren and dry. There's risk of heatstroke in the day and hypothermia at night. This desert was inhabited by antelope, wild donkeys, and lions, not to mention bandits and other desperados who sought refuge there. Yet all the accounts of the temptation say that Jesus was led or driven into the wilderness by the Holy Spirit. Clearly, this was a critical time of preparation for the road ahead.

The first temptation. In the Jordan River, Jesus heard the voice from heaven say, "You are my Son, the Beloved; with you I am well pleased" (Luke 3:22). In the desert, he is tempted to doubt this special relationship with the Father. "If you are the Son of God, command this stone to become a loaf of bread" (4:3).

We know Jesus is famished. Why not use his power to satisfy his own hunger? What harm would that do? But as we watch Jesus throughout his life, we learn that he doesn't use his power to serve his own needs—not once! His power was always directed toward serving the needs of others. And here in the desert he refuses to use miracles as proof that he is his Father's beloved Son. His answer to the tempter is, "It is written, 'One does not live by bread alone'" (v. 4).

The second temptation. The devil leads Jesus to a high mountain and, in a moment, displays to him all the world's kingdoms. "If you, then, will worship me, it will all be yours" (v. 7).

Notice that Jesus doesn't argue with Satan. He doesn't dispute the devil's claim that all the kingdoms belong to him. Jesus knows the truth of what the New Testament says in other places: Satan is the "ruler of this world," and he's the "ruler of the power of the air" (Eph. 2:2). But Jesus also knows something Satan has yet to discover—that his kingdom is a house of cards built on deception and fear and that it will one day collapse and come to nothing.

Still, this is a real temptation because conventional wisdom teaches us that in the world, you play by the world's rules. If you want to gain power and influence, you must master the arts of negotiation, compromise, and under-the-table dealing. But for Jesus to resort to these human strategies of personal kingdom building would mean selling his soul to the devil. Jesus is not about to bend his knee to Satan. He quotes Scripture again: "Worship the Lord your God, and serve only him" (Luke 4:7).

The third temptation. Jesus is transported to the pinnacle of the temple in Jerusalem. "If you are the Son of God, throw yourself down from here" (v. 9).

Why is this a temptation? Because the temple is the center of Jewish religious life. What a perfect place for Jesus to prove his special relationship with God! "God said he would protect you. So jump and make the angels catch you. Float down into the temple court and amaze the crowds. Stop hiding out in the desert; it's time to reveal your true identity, Son of God!"

But in the wilderness, Jesus has already settled the question. He will not force God's hand. He will not exploit his relationship with the Father. He doesn't do it here in the desert. He won't do it in Gethsemane when he can call thousands of angels to rescue him. And he won't do it when he hangs on the cross and hears the tempter's voice again (this time through the mouths of people mocking him), "If you are the Son of God, come down from the cross" (Matt. 27:40).

Jesus will not commit the sin of Israel in the desert when they tested God and asked, "Is the Lord among us or not?" (Exod. 17:7). He will not profane his relationship with God by performing religious stunts. So he quotes Scripture a third time: "It is said, 'Do not put the Lord your God to the test'" (Luke 4:12).

The evil one knows he is defeated, so he leaves Jesus "until an opportune time" (v. 13).

For many years, I thought the temptation in the wilderness was a case of the devil attacking Jesus when he was at his weakest point. But I've come to see that just the opposite is true. Jesus wasn't weak; he was strong. The enemy assumed this was a strategic time to attack, but he found out he was very wrong. This teaches us the importance of spiritual disciplines. Prayer, fasting, solitude, and meditation on Scripture—God used all these to pour strength into his Son so he would be ready for spiritual conflict. The temptations would continue throughout his life. But those weeks in the wilderness taught Jesus the Source of his strength.

"Then Jesus, filled with the power of the Spirit, returned to Galilee" (v. 14).

—Rick Power

After reading the passage from Luke 4:1-13 and the devotional reflection "A Wilderness Survival Guide," you may also want to read the following assigned passages:

Deuteronomy 26:1-11; Psalm 9:1-2, 9-16;
and Romans 10:8*b*-13

The discussion prompts that follow will help prepare you to participate in your Sunday school class or small-group study. Use your Reflective Journaling section to record any other insights that come to you as you read the gospel lesson and the devotional reflection.

DISCUSSION PROMPT NO. 1: LUKE 4:1-13

Luke tells us that Jesus was both "full of the Holy Spirit" and "led by the Spirit" and yet he faced temptation. What does this tell you about temptation in the life of the believer?

DISCUSSION PROMPT NO. 2: LUKE 4:1-13

The devil begins by challenging Jesus to turn stone into bread. How do our physical needs become opportunities for temptation to enter our lives?

DISCUSSION PROMPT NO. 3: LUKE 4:1-13

Jesus quoted scripture in response to each temptation (Deut. 8:3; 6:13; and 6:16). Which scriptures have been helpful to you when you faced temptation?

DISCUSSION PROMPT NO. 4: LUKE 4:1-13

Jesus was tempted to prove himself, "If you are the Son of God . . ." (vv. 3, 9). Have you ever felt tempted to prove yourself spiritually, "If you were a real Christian . . ."? How were you able to recognize the temptation? And, how did you respond?

DISCUSSION PROMPT NO. 5: DEVOTIONAL REFLECTION

In what ways will spiritual disciplines, such as prayer, fasting, and meditation on Scripture, strengthen us in times of temptation?

Reflective Journaling

MONDAY
WEEK 1 LENTEN SEASON

PSALM 19:7-14 • LEVITICUS 19:1-4, 11-18 • GALATIANS 1:1-5 • MATTHEW 25:31-46

MORNING MEDITATIONS

PRAYER—Father in heaven, at the baptism of Jesus in the River Jordan you proclaimed him your beloved Son and anointed him with the Holy Spirit. Grant that all who are baptized into his name may keep the covenant they have made, and boldly confess him as Lord and Savior. Amen.

PSALM 19:9b-10a, 11—The ordinances of the Lord are true and righteous altogether. More to be desired are they than gold, even much fine gold; sweeter also than honey . . . Moreover by them is your servant warned; in keeping them there is great reward.

LEVITICUS 19:1-2, 4   *You Shall Be Holy*
The Lord spoke to Moses, saying: Speak to all the congregation of the people of Israel and say to them: You shall be holy, for I the Lord your God am holy . . . Do not turn to idols or make cast images for yourselves: I am the Lord your God.

GALATIANS 1:3-4a   *God's Grace Has Been Given to You*
Grace to you and peace from God our Father and the Lord Jesus Christ, who gave himself for our sins to save us free from the present evil age.

MATTHEW 25:31-46   *Today's Gospel Reading*

> Set aside a place for yourself, separate from contact with other people so that your spiritual exercises won't be interrupted. Pure, devoted exercises nourish the soul with godly thoughts.
> ST. BASIL THE GREAT, *LETTER NO. 2*

EVENING REFLECTIONS

PSALM 44:3-4a—Not by their own sword did they win the land, nor did their own arm give them victory; but your right hand, and your arm, and the light of your countenance, for you delighted in them. You are my King and my God.

PRAYER—O God, give me grace to study your knowledge every day, so that the more I know you, the more I may love you. Create in me a zealous obedience to all your commands, a cheerful patience under your disciplines, and a thankful resignation to your will. Amen. **JW**

TUESDAY
WEEK 1 LENTEN SEASON

PSALM 34:4-7, 15-19 ▪ ISAIAH 55:10-11 ▪ GALATIANS 1:6-10 ▪ MATTHEW 6:5-15

MORNING MEDITATIONS

PRAYER—O Lord Jesus Christ, who created and redeemed me, and has brought me to this present moment, you know what you want to do with me; so, do with me according to your will, for your tender mercies' sake. Amen. ***King Henry VI***

PSALM 34:4, 6—I sought the Lord, and he answered me, and delivered me from all my fears . . . This poor soul cried, and was heard by the Lord, and was saved from every trouble.

ISAIAH 55:10a, 11 *My Word Shall Accomplish That Which I Purpose*
For as the rain and the snow come down from heaven, and do not return there until they have watered the earth . . . so shall my word be that goes out from my mouth; it shall not return to me empty, but it shall accomplish that which I purpose.

GALATIANS 1:6-7 *Some Want to Pervert the Gospel*
I am astonished that you are so quickly deserting the one who called you in the grace of Christ and are turning to a different gospel—not that there is another gospel, but there are some who are confusing you and want to pervert the gospel of Christ.

MATTHEW 6:5-15 *Today's Gospel Reading*

> If we lay open our hearts (that is if we confess our sins and make amends with God), we will be pardoned by Him who regards not the outward appearances, as people do, but the innermost secrets of the heart. ST. LACTANTIUS, *DIVINE INSTITUTES* 4

EVENING REFLECTIONS

PSALM 48:1, 9-10—Great is the Lord and greatly to be praised in the city of our God . . . We ponder your steadfast love, O God, in the midst of your temple. Your name, O God, like your praise, reaches to the ends of the earth.

PRAYER—Teach us, good Lord, to serve as you deserve; to give and not to count the cost; to fight and not to heed the wounds; to toil and not to seek for rest; to labor and not to ask for any reward, except that of knowing that we do your will; through Jesus Christ our Lord. Amen. ***St. Ignatius of Loyola***

WEDNESDAY
WEEK 1 LENTEN SEASON

PSALM 51:6-12 • AMOS 5:6-15 • GALATIANS 1:11-24 • LUKE 11:29-32

MORNING MEDITATIONS

PRAYER—Lord, how great is our dilemma! In your presence silence is best, but love inspires our hearts and urges us to speak. If we were to hold our peace, the stones would cry out; yet if we speak, what can we say? Teach us to know that we cannot know, for no one knows the things of God except the Spirit of God. So let faith support us where reason fails, and we shall think because we believe, not in order that we may believe. Amen. **A. W. Tozer**

PSALM 51:9-10—Hide your face from my sins, and blot out all my iniquities. Create in me a clean heart, O God, and put a new and right spirit within me.

AMOS 5:14-15a *Hate Evil, Love Good*
Seek good and not evil, that you may live; and so the Lord, the God of hosts, will be with you, just as you have said. Hate evil and love good, and establish justice.

GALATIANS 1:11 *The Gospel Is Not from Human Origin*
For I want you to know . . . that the gospel that was proclaimed by me is not from human origin; for I did not receive it from a human source, nor was I taught it, but I received it through a revelation of Jesus Christ.

LUKE 11:29-32 *Today's Gospel Reading*

> "Peter, lovest thou Me?" When Peter confessed that he did, the Lord added, "If thou lovest Me tend my sheep." The Master did not ask the disciple if he loved Him in order to get information (why would He when He already knows everyone's heart?), but to teach us how great an interest He has in the care of these sheep.   ST. CHRYSOSTOM, *TREATISE NO. 2*

EVENING REFLECTIONS

PSALM 53:1-2—Fools say in their hearts, "There is no God." They are corrupt, they commit abominable acts; there is no one who does good. God looks down from heaven on humankind to see if there are any who are wise, who seek after God.

PRAYER—O God, you are the giver of all good gifts and I desire to praise your name for all of your goodness to me. I thank you for sending your Son to die for my sins, for the means of grace, and for the hope of glory, through Jesus Christ. Amen. **JW**

THURSDAY
WEEK I — LENTEN SEASON

PSALM 138 ▪ ESTHER 4 ▪ GALATIANS 2:1-10 ▪ MATTHEW 7:7-12

MORNING MEDITATIONS

PRAYER—Lord of all! You are the great IAM. Yet I confess, made in your image, I can repeat "I am," and in that confession acknowledge that I derive from you . . . You are the great Original of which we through your goodness are grateful if imperfect copies. I worship you, O Father everlasting! **A. W. Tozer**

PSALM 138:7-8—Though I walk in the midst of trouble, you preserve me against the wrath of my enemies; you stretch out your hand, and your right hand delivers me. The Lord will fulfill his purpose for me; your steadfast love, O Lord, endures forever.

ESTHER 4:13-14   *For Such a Time as This*
Mordecai told them to reply to Esther, "Do not think that in the king's palace you will escape . . . For if you keep silence at such a time as this, relief and deliverance will rise for the Jews from another quarter . . . Who knows? Perhaps you have come to royal dignity for just such a time as this."

GALATIANS 2:9b-10   *Remember the Poor*
They gave to Barnabas and me the right hand of fellowship, agreeing that we should go to the Gentiles . . . They asked only one thing, that we remember the poor, which was actually what I was eager to do.

MATTHEW 7:7-12   *Today's Gospel Reading*

> Those who by God's gracious gift have become his children, born again from above of his Holy Spirit, possessing Christ within themselves to illuminate and recreate them, are guided in the many and varied ways of the Spirit, as grace works in their hearts invisibly and in peace of soul.
> — ANONYMOUS, *4TH CENTURY, HOMILY 18*

EVENING REFLECTIONS

PSALM 59:16-17—But I will sing of your might; I will sing aloud of your steadfast love . . . For you have been . . . a refuge in the day of my distress. O my strength, I will sing praises to you, for you, O God, are my fortress, the God who shows me steadfast love.

PRAYER—O Lord, I want to offer an evening sacrifice, the sacrifice of a contrite spirit. Have mercy on me, O God, according to your great goodness and the multitude of your mercies. Cleanse me from all filthiness of flesh and spirit that I may follow you with a pure heart and mind. Amen. **JW**

FRIDAY — WEEK 1, LENTEN SEASON

PSALM 130 • EZEKIEL 18:21-32 • GALATIANS 2:11-16 • MATTHEW 5:21-26

MORNING MEDITATIONS

PRAYER—Eternal God, the light of the minds that know you, the joy of the hearts that love you and the strength of the wills that serve you; grant us so to know you that we may truly love you, so to love you that we may truly serve you, whom to serve is perfect freedom; through Jesus Christ our Lord. Amen. **St. Augustine**

PSALM 130:1-4—Out of the depths I cry to you, O Lord. Lord, hear my voice! Let your ears be attentive to the voice of my supplications! If you, O Lord, should mark iniquities, Lord, who could stand? But there is forgiveness with you, so that you may be revered.

EZEKIEL 18:21-22a *No Transgressions Shall Be Remembered*
But if the wicked turn away from all their sins that they have committed and keep all my statutes and do what is lawful and right, they shall surely live; they shall not die. None of the transgressions that they have committed shall be remembered against them.

GALATIANS 2:16 *Justified by Faith in Christ*
We know that a person is justified not by the works of the law but through faith in Jesus Christ. And we have come to believe in Christ Jesus, so that we might be justified by faith in Christ, and not by doing the works of the law.

MATTHEW 5:21-26 *Today's Gospel Reading*

> Let us pray diligently. Prayer is a mighty weapon if used with earnestness and sincerity, without drawing attention to ourselves . . . We need much repentance, beloved, much prayer, much endurance, and much perseverance to gain the good things that have been promised to us. ST. CHRYSOSTOM, *HOMILY 27 ON HEBREWS*

EVENING REFLECTIONS

PSALM 54:1-2—Save me, O God, by your name, and vindicate me by your might. Hear my prayer, O God; give ear to the words of my mouth.

PRAYER—Steer the ship of my life, good Lord, to your quiet harbor, where I can be safe from the storms of sin and conflict . . . Renew in me the gift of discernment, so that I can always see the right path that I should steer. And give me the strength and courage to choose the right course, even when the sea is rough and the waves are high, knowing that through enduring hardship and danger I shall find comfort and peace. **St. Basil of Caesarea**

SATURDAY
WEEK I — LENTEN SEASON

PSALM 119:1-8 • DEUTERONOMY 26:16-19 • GALATIANS 2:19-21 • MATTHEW 5:43-48

MORNING MEDITATIONS

PRAYER—Take, Lord, all my liberty, my memory, my understanding and my whole will. You have given me all that I have, all that I am, and I surrender all to your divine will. Give me only your love and your grace. With this I am rich enough, and I have no more to ask. In Jesus' name. Amen. *St. Ignatius of Loyola*

PSALM 119:4-6—You have commanded your precepts to be kept diligently. O that my ways may be steadfast in keeping your statutes! Then I shall not be put to shame, having fixed my eyes on all your commandments.

DEUTERONOMY 26:18, 19b *Keep His Commandments*
Today the LORD has obtained your agreement: to be his treasured people, as he promised you, to keep his commandments . . . for you to be a people holy to the LORD your God, as he promised.

GALATIANS 2:20 *I Live by Faith in the Son of God*
It is no longer I who live, but it is Christ who lives in me. And the life I now live in the flesh I live by faith in the Son of God, who loved me and gave himself for me.

MATTHEW 5:43-48 *Today's Gospel Reading*

> Now Christ is formed in a believer through faith implanted in his inmost soul. Such a one, gentle and lowly of heart, is summoned to the freedom of grace, and he does not boast of the merit of works which are of no value . . . [rather he] cleaves to Christ with spiritual love.
> ST. AUGUSTINE, *AN EXPLANATION OF THE LETTER TO THE GALATIANS, NO. 37-38*

EVENING REFLECTIONS

PSALM 139:17-18—How weighty to me are your thoughts, O God! How vast is the sum of them! I try to count them—they are more than the sand; I come to the end—I am still with you.

PRAYER—Merciful Father, accept my sincere thanks and praise for life and every other blessing of your grace. You have redeemed me by your blood and sanctified me by the grace of your Holy Spirit. For these and all other mercies, I praise and magnify your glorious name. Amen. *JW*

WEEK TWO
*L*ENTEN *S*EASON

Sunday: Jerusalem, Jerusalem!

Read the gospel passage from Luke 13:31-35 and the
devotional reflection titled "Jerusalem, Jerusalem!"
then respond to the discussion prompts
in the Reflective Journaling section.

THE MUSIC OF ASHES TO FIRE

Week 2: "See the Kingdom Coming" (Track 3)

Monday through Saturday

IN THE MORNING:

A personal daily devotional guide includes prayer,
a reading from the Old Testament, the Psalms, the Epistles,
and the Gospels for each day of the week.

In addition to the daily psalm, this week's readings come from
Daniel, Isaiah, Jeremiah, Genesis, Micah, Galatians,
and the gospels of Matthew and Luke.

Inspirational quotes from men and women of faith
keep us in contact with our shared Christian heritage.

IN THE EVENING:

An evening psalm and prayer become preludes
to nighttime rest and renewal.

Lenten Season—Week Two
Jerusalem, Jerusalem!

A devotional reflection based on Luke 13:31-35

Read the gospel passage first, then the devotional reflection that follows. The discussion prompts at the end will help prepare you for Sunday school and small-group sessions.

"Jerusalem, Jerusalem, the city that kills the prophets and stones those who are sent to it! How often have I desired to gather your children together as a hen gathers her brood under her wings, and you were not willing!" (Luke 13:34).

Traditionally this statement is understood as a lament—an expression of tearful grief. The image of a weeping Jesus is rare in Scripture and requires us to ask, "What is it that moves the heart of God?"

As a small boy, I recall tuning out the majority of the testimony services in our little church on the South Dakota prairie. In most of those Wednesday evening services the same phrases seemed to come from the same people who were always the first to stand when given the opportunity. But once in a while something rare would happen. My mother would stand and begin tearfully to confess her dependence amid life's difficulties on a faithful and loving God. And to this day, when I hear the humble tremble in my mother's voice and see the tears flow down her face, I can't help but respond with my own tears. There is something so intimate, so heart-wrenching, so powerful and moving about my mother's tears.

As we witness the lament of Jesus in Luke, we are moved to wonder why Jesus was calling out to Jerusalem so passionately. What was it that moved Jesus to tears? Jerusalem had come to symbolize a people who rejected and ultimately killed those whom God had sent them. Their rejection of God's leading was steering them to their own destruction.

Jesus was grieving simply because Jerusalem (representing the whole people of Israel) had missed the heart of his teaching and, in so doing, the heart of God. They had the wrong *expectations* about him. They had accepted the idea of a loving God but rejected the command to love their neighbors. They had accepted the idea of a ruling king but rejected the reality of a forever-reigning Messiah. They were blind to the reality that God was keeping his promise and once again sending them a prophet, and this time someone more than a prophet—his own Son.

It is interesting that Jesus' words recorded in Luke are identical to his words recorded in Matthew's gospel (23:37). But in Matthew, rather than lamenting over Jerusalem during his *journey to Jerusalem*, Jesus is recorded as lamenting during his last week of life *while in Jerusalem*. In Matthew, Jesus' lament came on the heels of his challenging the hypocritical religious leaders, those who knew the Scriptures but ignored the more important matters of the law—"justice and mercy and faith" (v. 23). Perhaps Matthew's rendition gives us an insight into what breaks the heart of God—injustice, cruelty, and broken promises.

Here is where I have to inject the reality that is found among many of our churches today. Jesus' words could easily speak directly to us: "Church, church, the community that kills the pastors and stones the ones sent to it. How I long to see you united as one. I left you with a job to do. So I tell you again, you will not see me until you can live out the love and peace I modeled for you."

Jerusalem was on the mind of Jesus for good reason; it reflected the heart of the whole people of Israel. The church is on our minds for good reason; it is God's representative in the world. As the church, we represent the practices of God's people in God's world. We are asked to participate in what God started in Jesus—the salvation of the world. Where there is brokenness, we are called to bring reconciliation. Where there is oppression, we are called to bring freedom. Where there is spiritual blindness, we are called to bring understanding. We, too, are challenged to see justice, mercy, and faithfulness as our high calling.

In many ways the reputation of the church today parallels the reputation of Jerusalem. Too often we settle for rote testimonies or a dry religion of rules. We sprinkle a little Jesus conversation on top of our lives and check off the spiritual to-do list once a week. We, too, have become influenced by a stone-throwing culture that is quick to become angry, eager to reject the hurting, and determined to break covenant with those who think differently. We need to witness the tears of Jesus once again.

Unfortunately, the people of Jerusalem weren't moved and changed by the words of Jesus. But this isn't the end of the story. The connection of this passage to Luke 24:47 cannot be ignored. After Jesus enlightens the minds of the disciples about the meaning of the Scriptures, he tells them that "repentance and forgiveness of sins is to be proclaimed in his name to all nations, beginning from Jerusalem" (v. 47).

Jerusalem was given another chance. Our opportunity is still in front of us. The world is still waiting. We must be a people passionate for *justice*, motivated by *mercy*, and committed to being *faithful* representatives of our covenant-keeping God.

How will you respond to the tears of Jesus? —Shane Ash

After reading the passage from Luke 13:31-35 and the devotional reflection "Jerusalem, Jerusalem!" you may also want to read the following related passages:

Genesis 15:1-12, 17-18; Psalm 27; Philippians 3:17—4:1

The discussion prompts that follow will help prepare you to participate in your Sunday school class or small-group study. Use your Reflective Journaling section to record any other insights that come to you as you read the gospel lesson and the devotional reflection.

DISCUSSION PROMPT NO. 1: LUKE 13:31-35

What do you think Jesus meant by "on the third day I finish my work" (v. 32)?

DISCUSSION PROMPT NO. 2: LUKE 13:31-35

Jesus said, "I must be on my way" (v. 33). In what ways have threats or fears taken your focus off God's plan for your life? How did you regain it?

DISCUSSION PROMPT NO. 3: LUKE 13:31-35

What was it that kept Jerusalem from experiencing God's protection and care? In what ways can believers avoid being caught in the same fate?

DISCUSSION PROMPT NO. 4: LUKE 13:31-35

"Blessed is the one who comes in the name of the Lord" (v. 35) foretold what event in the life of Jesus? How does acknowledging Jesus allow us to "see" him clearly?

DISCUSSION PROMPT NO. 5: DEVOTIONAL REFLECTION

Many in Jesus' day missed the heart of his teaching because they had the wrong expectations. In what ways can we avoid developing wrong expectations about what God wants to do in our lives?

Reflective Journaling

MONDAY | WEEK 2 LENTEN SEASON

PSALM 79:8-13 • DANIEL 9:4b-19 • GALATIANS 3:1-14 • LUKE 6:32-38

MORNING MEDITATIONS

PRAYER—Lord God, send your Holy Spirit to be the guide of all my ways and the sanctifier of my soul and body. Give me the light of your presence, your peace from heaven, and the salvation of my soul, through Jesus Christ my Lord. Amen. *JW*

PSALM 79:9—Help us, O God of our salvation, for the glory of your name; deliver us, and forgive our sins, for your name's sake.

DANIEL 9:4b-5, 19 *We Have Sinned*
Ah, Lord, great and awesome God, keeping covenant and steadfast love with those who love you and keep your commandments, we have sinned and done wrong, acted wickedly and rebelled, turning aside from your commandments and ordinances . . . O Lord, hear; O Lord, forgive; O Lord, listen and act.

GALATIANS 3:13-14 *Christ Redeemed Us from the Curse*
Christ redeemed us from the curse of the law by becoming a curse for us—for it is written, "Cursed is everyone who hangs on a tree"—in order that in Christ Jesus the blessing of Abraham might come to the Gentiles, so that we might receive the promise of the Spirit through faith.

LUKE 6:32-38 *Today's Gospel Reading*

> My son, hear my words, words most sweet, excelling all the learning of philosophers and the wise men of this world. My words are spirit and life and are not to be weighed by human standards . . . Write my words in your heart, and think diligently on them; for they will be very necessary in the time of temptation.
>
> THOMAS À KEMPIS, *THE IMITATION OF CHRIST*

EVENING REFLECTIONS

PSALM 65:1-3—Praise is due to you, O God, in Zion; and to you shall vows be performed, O you who answer prayer! To you all flesh shall come. When deeds of iniquity overwhelm us, you forgive our transgressions.

PRAYER (PSALM 51:17, 7)—O Lord, "the sacrifice acceptable to [you] is a broken spirit; a broken and contrite heart, O God, you will not despise . . . Purge me with hyssop, and I shall be clean; wash me, and I shall be whiter than snow." Amen.

TUESDAY
WEEK 2 — LENTEN SEASON

PSALM 50:1-15, 22-23 ▪ ISAIAH 1:10-20 ▪ GALATIANS 3:15-18 ▪ MATTHEW 23:1-12

MORNING MEDITATIONS

PRAYER—I pray, O God, to know you, to love you, that I may rejoice in you. And if I cannot attain to full joy in this life may I at least advance from day to day, until that joy shall come to the full. Amen. **St. Anselm**

PSALM 50:1-3a, 14—The mighty one, God the LORD, speaks and summons the earth from the rising of the sun to its setting. Out of Zion, the perfection of beauty, God shines forth. Our God comes and does not keep silence . . . Offer to God a sacrifice of thanksgiving, and pay your vows to the Most High.

ISAIAH 1:16-18a *Your Sins Shall Be as Snow*
Wash yourselves; make yourselves clean; remove the evil of your doings from before my eyes; cease to do evil, learn to do good; seek justice, rescue the oppressed, defend the orphan, plead for the widow. Come now, let us argue it out, says the LORD; though your sins are like scarlet, they shall be like snow.

GALATIANS 3:16a, c *Promise Fulfilled*
Now the promises were made to Abraham and to his offspring . . . that is, to one person, who is Christ.

MATTHEW 23:1-12 *Today's Gospel Reading*

> Learn to know the dignity of your nature. Remember that image of God in which you were created, which, though defaced by Adam, is now restored in Christ . . . Let us listen to the Apostle's words, "For you have died and your life is hid with Christ in God. When Christ who is our life appears, then you also will appear with him in glory."
>
> ST. LEO THE GREAT, *SERMON 7*

EVENING REFLECTIONS

PSALM 84:11-12—For the LORD God is a sun and shield; he bestows favor and honor. No good thing does the LORD withhold from those who walk uprightly. O LORD of hosts, happy is everyone who trusts in you.

PRAYER (PSALM 51:17, 10)—O Lord, "the sacrifice acceptable to [you] is a broken spirit; a broken and contrite heart, O God, you will not despise . . . Create in me a clean heart, O God, and put a new and right spirit within me." Amen.

WEDNESDAY
WEEK 2 LENTEN SEASON

PSALM 31:1-16 ▪ JEREMIAH 18:18-20 ▪ GALATIANS 3:19-29 ▪ MATTHEW 20:17-28

MORNING MEDITATIONS

PRAYER—O God, you are the giver of all good gifts and I desire to praise your name for all of your goodness to me. I thank you for sending your Son to die for my sins, for the means of grace, and for the hope of glory, through Jesus Christ. Amen. **JW**

PSALM 31:14-15—But I trust in you, O Lord; I say, "You are my God." My times are in your hand; deliver me from the hand of my enemies and persecutors. Let your face shine upon your servant; save me in your steadfast love.

JEREMIAH 18:19-20a *Give Heed to Me, O Lord*
Give heed to me, O Lord, and listen to what my adversaries say! Is evil a recompense for good? Yet they have dug a pit for my life.

GALATIANS 3:25-27 *Children of God through Faith*
But now that faith has come, we are no longer subject to a disciplinarian, for in Christ Jesus you are all children of God through faith. As many of you as were baptized into Christ have clothed yourself with Christ.

MATTHEW 20:17-28 *Today's Gospel Reading*

> How precious is the gift of the cross . . . For it is a tree which brings forth life, not death. It is the source of light, not darkness. It offers you a home in Eden. It does not cast you out. It is the tree which Christ mounted, and so destroyed the devil, and rescued the human race from slavery to the tyrant.
>
> ST. THEODORE THE STUDITE, *ON THE ADORATION OF THE CROSS*

EVENING REFLECTIONS

PSALM 29:1-2, 11—Ascribe to the Lord, O heavenly beings, ascribe to the Lord glory and strength. Ascribe to the Lord the glory of his name; worship the Lord in holy splendor . . . May the Lord give strength to his people! May the Lord bless his people with peace.

PRAYER (PSALM 51:17, 12)—O Lord, "the sacrifice acceptable to [you] is a broken spirit; a broken and contrite heart, O God, you will not despise . . . Restore to me the joy of your salvation, and sustain in me a willing spirit." Amen.

THURSDAY
WEEK 2
LENTEN SEASON

PSALM 15 ▪ JEREMIAH 17:5-10 ▪ GALATIANS 4:1-7 ▪ LUKE 16:19-31

MORNING MEDITATIONS

PRAYER—My Lord, open my eyes to behold your presence and strengthen my hands to do your will, that the world may rejoice and give you praise. Blessed are you, Sovereign God of all, to you be praise and glory forever. Amen. *JW*

PSALM 15:1-2—O Lord, who may abide in your tent? Who may dwell on your holy hill? Those who walk blamelessly, and do what is right, and speak the truth from their heart.

JEREMIAH 17:9-10 *The Lord Tests the Mind*
The heart is devious above all else; it is perverse—who can understand it? I the Lord test the mind and search the heart, to give to all according to their ways, according to the fruit of their doings.

GALATIANS 4:4-5 *God Sent His Son*
But when the fullness of time had come, God sent his Son, born of a woman, born under the law, in order to redeem those who were under the law, so that we might receive adoption as children.

LUKE 16:19-31 *Today's Gospel Reading*

> Just as the Father is seen in the Son, so the Son is seen in the Holy Spirit. Worship in the Spirit suggests the activity of our intelligence . . . Our Lord said that we must worship in Spirit and in truth, and by "truth" he clearly meant himself. We speak of worship in the Son, which is worship in the one who is the image of God the Father.
>
> ST. BASIL THE GREAT, *ON THE HOLY SPIRIT*

EVENING REFLECTIONS

PSALM 70:4-5—Let all who seek you rejoice and be glad in you. Let those who love your salvation say evermore, "God is great!" But I am poor and needy; hasten to me, O God! You are my help and my deliverer; O Lord, do not delay!

PRAYER (PSALM 51:17, 6)—O Lord, "the sacrifice acceptable to [you] is a broken spirit; a broken and contrite heart, O God, you will not despise . . . You desire truth in the inward being; therefore teach me wisdom in my secret heart." Amen.

FRIDAY
WEEK 2 LENTEN SEASON

PSALM 105:7-22 ▪ GENESIS 37:1-4, 12-28 ▪ GALATIANS 4:8-20 ▪ MATTHEW 21:33-43

MORNING MEDITATIONS

PRAYER—I do not endeavor, O Lord, to penetrate your sublimity, for in no wise do I compare my understanding with that; but I long to understand in some degree your truth, which my heart believes and loves. **St. Anselm**

PSALM 105:7-9a—He is the Lord our God; his judgments are in all the earth. He is mindful of his covenant forever, of the word that he commanded, for a thousand generations, the covenant that he made with Abraham.

GENESIS 37:28 *They Took Joseph to Egypt*
When some Midianite traders passed by, they drew Joseph up, lifting him out of the pit, and sold him to the Ishmaelites for twenty pieces of silver. And they took Joseph to Egypt.

GALATIANS 4:8-9a *Don't Turn Back*
Formerly, when you did not know God, you were enslaved to beings that by nature are not gods. Now, however, that you have come to know God, or rather to be known by God, how can you turn back?

MATTHEW 21:33-43 *Today's Gospel Reading*

> Hope is the power that drives love. Thanks to hope, we can look forward to the reward of charity . . . Hope is the doorway of love . . . The absence of hope destroys charity; our efforts are bound to it, our labors are sustained by it, and through it we are enveloped by the mercy of God. ST. JOHN CLIMACUS, *LADDER OF DIVINE ASCENT*

EVENING REFLECTIONS

PSALM 73:23, 26—I am continually with you; you hold my right hand. You guide me with your counsel, and afterward you will receive me with honor. Whom have I in heaven but you? And there is nothing on earth that I desire other than you . . . God is the strength of my heart.

PRAYER (PSALM 51:17, 11)—O Lord, "the sacrifice acceptable to [you] is a broken spirit; a broken and contrite heart, O God, you will not despise . . . Do not cast me away from your presence, and do not take your holy spirit from me." Amen.

SATURDAY
WEEK 2 — LENTEN SEASON

PSALM 103:1-5, 10-14 ▪ **MICAH 7:14-20** ▪ **GALATIANS 4:21—5:1** ▪ **LUKE 15:1-3, 11-32**

MORNING MEDITATIONS

PRAYER—Lord, I do not seek to understand that I may believe, but I believe in order to understand. For this also I believe, that unless I believed, I should not understand. ***St. Anselm***

PSALM 103:2-5—Bless the Lord, O my soul, and do not forget all his benefits—who forgives all your iniquity, who heals all your diseases, who redeems your life from the Pit, who crowns you with steadfast love and mercy, who satisfies you with good as long as you live so that your youth is renewed like the eagle's.

MICAH 7:15, 16a, 17bc *Show Us Marvelous Things*
As in the days when you came out of the land of Egypt, show us marvelous things. The nations shall be ashamed . . . they shall come trembling out of their fortresses; they shall turn in dread to the Lord our God and they shall stand in fear of you.

GALATIANS 5:1 *Don't Submit to a Yoke of Slavery*
For freedom Christ has set us free. Stand firm, therefore, and do not submit again to a yoke of slavery.

LUKE 15:1-3, 11-32 *Today's Gospel Reading*

> We must be in God, and live in him and cling to him, for he is beyond all human thought and understanding and he dwells in endless peace and tranquility. This peace passes all understanding, passes all perception. — ST. AMBROSE, ON FLIGHT FROM THE WORLD

EVENING REFLECTIONS

PSALM 23:6—Surely goodness and mercy shall follow me all the days of my life, and I shall dwell in the house of the Lord my whole life long.

PRAYER (PSALM 51:17, 7)—O Lord, "the sacrifice acceptable to [you] is a broken spirit; a broken and contrite heart, O God, you will not despise . . . Purge me with hyssop, and I shall be clean; wash me, and I shall be whiter than snow." Amen.

WEEK THREE
Lenten Season

Sunday: About-Face—Beautiful!

Read the gospel passage from Luke 13:1-9 and
the devotional reflection titled "About-Face—Beautiful!"
then respond to the discussion prompts
in the Reflective Journaling section.

THE MUSIC OF ASHES TO FIRE
Week 3: "Beautiful" (Track 4)

Monday through Saturday

IN THE MORNING:

A personal daily devotional guide includes prayer,
a reading from the Old Testament, the Psalms, the Epistles,
and the Gospels for each day of the week.

In addition to the daily psalm, this week's readings come from
2 Kings, Daniel, Deuteronomy, Jeremiah, Hosea, Galatians,
2 John, and the gospels of Matthew, Mark, and Luke.

Inspirational quotes from men and women of faith
keep us in contact with our shared Christian heritage.

IN THE EVENING:

An evening psalm and prayer become preludes
to nighttime rest and renewal.

SUNDAY

Lenten Season—Week Three
About-Face—Beautiful!

A devotional reflection based on Luke 13:1-9

Read the gospel passage first, then the devotional reflection that follows. The discussion prompts at the end will help prepare you for Sunday school and small-group sessions.

Forty years ago, I graduated from Charlotte Hall Military Academy. Located in Charlotte Hall, Maryland, the school was founded in 1774, making it, until its closing in 1976, one of the oldest private military academies in continuous operation in the United States.

One of the first things a cadet was required to learn was how to perform an about-face. Our drill instructor, retired Army Sergeant Major Robert Schulton, made sure every cadet knew how to execute an about-face properly. If you didn't execute the command perfectly, you got an earful from this salty old veteran, who was, before his retirement, the highest ranking noncommissioned officer in the army and a Bataan Death March and POW camp survivor!

An about-face is a drill command and is, quite frankly, no easy maneuver. It requires skill, coordination, and timing. From the position of attention, and on the command "About-face," a soldier is to place the right foot a few inches behind the other, turn around 180 degrees (and so face the opposite direction), and end with the feet in the original position, 45 degrees apart. It's tricky! But honestly, when an entire unit or company executes an about-face together, it's a wonderful thing to watch. There's a certain grace and beauty to it.

Interestingly, the word "repentance" is the English translation of the Greek word *metanoia*. *Metanoia* is often understood to mean a "change of mind" or a "change of heart." But a close look reveals that *metanoia* may be understood as a military term, a command that clearly means to do an about-face—to turn away from the old way of living and thinking and face a new direction. And apparently this change of mind and heart, away from the things of this world and to the things of God, is required. It is a command. It is not an option. In fact, Luke reports Jesus saying that we have but two options—repent or perish (see 13:3). The confession of one's sins is a great start: "If we confess our sins, he who is faithful and just will forgive us our sins and cleanse us from all unrighteousness" (1 John 1:9).

But confession must be followed by repentance. "Unless you repent, you will all perish," said Jesus (Luke 13:5). There is no ambiguity here. Kingdom people repent. One cannot become a true Christ follower without repentance, and one cannot remain in close fellowship with the company of the committed without continued repentance.

Repentance is, after all, Jesus' first doctrinal statement: "Repent, for the kingdom of heaven has come near" (Matt. 4:17). To illustrate the importance of repentance, Jesus told a parable about a fig tree that bore no fruit (Luke 13:6-9). No fruit? Then cut it down. The point? The truly repentant person is a fruit-bearing tree. Without the fruit of repentance dangling from the branches of one's life, conversion—life change—has not taken effect.

As a pastor, I've witnessed many a prayer of confession. "God, I'm sorry. I agree with you that I'm a sinner and that I need your forgiving grace." Truly that is a wonderful start. But unless that confession is followed by a genuine, grace-enabled heart change and life change, unless (as Paul suggests in 2 Cor. 5:17, KJV) "old things [begin to pass] away" and "all things . . . become new," there's not much in the way of fruit on the tree, is there?

Lent is as good a time as any for the church to perform an about-face or two. Let's practice this together under the direction of the Holy Spirit. When a church becomes a repentant community, well—it's a thing of beauty and grace. So let's become a company of the committed and together listen to the Spirit's direction: "About-face!"

> Do we fail to search the Scriptures? About-face!
> Are we forgetting to pray? About-face!
> Is our stewardship poor? About-face!
> Do we possess a bitter spirit? About-face!
> Are our habits undisciplined? About-face!
> Do we gossip? About-face!
> Is agape missing from our fellowship? About-face!
> Are we neglecting our mission? About-face!

When we are together, as the church of Jesus, and begin again to obey the commands of the Spirit, when we do an *about-face*—well, it's a beautiful thing to watch!
—Bud Reedy

After reading the passage from Luke 13:1-9 and the devotional reflection "About-Face—Beautiful!" you may also want to read the following related passages:

Isaiah 55:1-9; Psalm 63:1-8; 1 Corinthians 10:1-13

The discussion prompts that follow will help prepare you to participate in your Sunday school class or small-group study. Use your Reflective Journaling section to record any other insights that come to you as you read the gospel lesson and the devotional reflection.

DISCUSSION PROMPT NO. 1: LUKE 13:1-9

What does Jesus' question—"Do you think that . . . they were worse sinners?" (v. 2)—tell us about his attitude toward those who died as a result of brutality or tragedy?

DISCUSSION PROMPT NO. 2: LUKE 13:1-9

Why do you think Jesus warns his hearers, "But unless you repent, you will all perish" (v. 3)? Do you think he was talking about physical death only?

DISCUSSION PROMPT NO. 3: LUKE 13:1-9

Why does the vineyard owner command that the fig tree be cut down? How is this similar to Jesus' warning in John 15:1-8?

DISCUSSION PROMPT NO. 4: LUKE 13:1-9

The vineyard caretaker pleads with the owner to allow him one more year to make the tree productive. How is this like God's mercy in our lives?

DISCUSSION PROMPT NO. 5: DEVOTIONAL REFLECTION

What practical implications might the purging of the temple have for twenty-first-century believers?

REFLECTIVE JOURNALING

MONDAY | WEEK 3 LENTEN SEASON

PSALM 42:1-8 ▪ 2 KINGS 5:1-15b ▪ GALATIANS 5:2-15 ▪ LUKE 4:24-30

MORNING MEDITATIONS

PRAYER—Our Father in heaven, hallowed be your Name, your kingdom come, your will be done, on earth as it is in heaven. Give us today our daily bread. Forgive us our sins as we forgive those who sin against us. Save us from the time of trial, and deliver us from evil. For the kingdom, the power, and the glory are yours, now and for ever. Amen. **BCP**

PSALM 42:1-2—As a deer longs for flowing streams, so my soul longs for you, O God. My soul thirsts for God, for the living God.

2 KINGS 5:14-15b *His Flesh Was Restored*
So he went down and immersed himself seven times in the Jordan, according to the word of the man of God; his flesh was restored like the flesh of a young boy, and he was clean. Then he returned to the man of God . . . and said, "Now I know that there is no God in all the earth except in Israel."

GALATIANS 5:13-14 *You Were Called to Freedom*
For you were called to freedom, brothers and sisters; only do not use your freedom as an opportunity for self-indulgence, but through love become slaves to one another. For the whole law is summed up in a single commandment, "You shall love your neighbor as yourself."

LUKE 4:24-30 *Today's Gospel Reading*

> Service to Christ may not be performed easily. It may involve self-denial and labor, misunderstanding and sorrow, hardship and heartache. But it will result in a sense of accomplishment with a deep sense of inner satisfaction.   E. S. MANN, *THE THINGS THAT COUNT*

EVENING REFLECTIONS

PSALM 34:8-9, 10b—O taste and see that the LORD is good; happy are those who take refuge in him. O fear the LORD, you his holy ones, for those who fear him have no want . . . those who seek the LORD lack no good thing.

PRAYER—O Lamb of God, in this evening sacrifice of praise and prayer, I offer you a contrite heart. Give me grace, throughout my whole life, in every thought, and word, and work to imitate your meekness and humility, through Christ, my Lord, I pray. Amen. **JW**

TUESDAY — WEEK 3, LENTEN SEASON

PSALM 17:1-8 ▪ DANIEL 3:24-25, 28—4:3 ▪ GALATIANS 5:16-21 ▪ MATTHEW 18:21-35

MORNING MEDITATIONS

PRAYER—Our Father in heaven, hallowed be your Name, **your kingdom come, your will be done, on earth as it is in heaven.** Give us today our daily bread. Forgive us our sins as we forgive those who sin against us. Save us from the time of trial, and deliver us from evil. For the kingdom, the power, and the glory are yours, now and for ever. Amen. ***BCP***

PSALM 17:6-8—I will call upon you, for you will answer me, O God; incline your ear to me, hear my words. Wondrously show your steadfast love, O savior of those who seek refuge . . . at your right hand. Guard me as the apple of the eye; hide me in the shadow of your wings.

DANIEL 4:1a, 2-3 *Mighty Are His Wonders*
King Nebuchadnezzar to all peoples . . . The signs and wonders that the Most High God has worked for me I am pleased to recount. How great are his signs, how mighty are his wonders! His kingdom is an everlasting kingdom, and his sovereignty is from generation to generation.

GALATIANS 5:16-17ab *Live by the Spirit*
Live by the Spirit, I say, and do not gratify the desires of the flesh. For what the flesh desires is opposed to the Spirit, and what the Spirit desires is opposed to the flesh.

MATTHEW 18:21-35 *Today's Gospel Reading*

> When one has met Christ, dreams become inspired. The daily walk with Christ gives life its meaning. A Christ-centered, Christ-controlled, Christ-directed life creates significance in the midst of the pressures of our day.
>
> E. S. MANN, *THE THINGS THAT COUNT*

EVENING REFLECTIONS

PSALM 77:11-13—I will call to mind the deeds of the LORD; I will remember your wonders of old. I will meditate on all your work, and muse on your mighty deeds. Your way, O God, is holy. What god is so great as our God?

PRAYER—Almighty God, help me to proclaim your saving power in all I say and do. Protect me through the night and when I awake, enlighten my mind and enkindle my heart to think and love more like Jesus, your Son. ***JW***

WEDNESDAY
WEEK 3 LENTEN SEASON

PSALM 147:12-20 ▪ **DEUTERONOMY 4:1, 5-9** ▪ **GALATIANS 5:22-26** ▪ **MATTHEW 5:17-20**

MORNING MEDITATIONS

PRAYER—Our Father in heaven, hallowed be your Name, your kingdom come, your will be done, on earth as it is in heaven. **Give us today our daily bread.** Forgive us our sins as we forgive those who sin against us. Save us from the time of trial, and deliver us from evil. For the kingdom, the power, and the glory are yours, now and for ever. Amen. **BCP**

PSALM 147:12-13—Praise the LORD, O Jerusalem! Praise your God, O Zion! For he strengthens the bars of your gates; he blesses your children within you.

DEUTERONOMY 4:9 *Take Care*
Take care and watch yourselves closely, so as neither to forget the things that your eyes have seen nor to let them slip from your mind all the days of your life; make them known to your children and your children's children.

GALATIANS 5:22-23, 25 *Let Us Be Guided by the Spirit*
The fruit of the Spirit is love, joy, peace, patience, kindness, generosity, faithfulness, gentleness, and self-control. There is no law against such things . . . If we live by the Spirit, let us also be guided by the Spirit.

MATTHEW 5:17-20 *Today's Gospel Reading*

> Always go the second mile—willingly; trust God to work all things for your good, eventually; devote your energies to Christ and the upbuilding of his kingdom, unceasingly. Accept the torch of abundant Christian living, lighted at the altar of faith.
>
> <div align="right">E. S. MANN, <i>THE THINGS THAT COUNT</i></div>

EVENING REFLECTIONS

PSALM 82:3-4a, 8a—Give justice to the weak and the orphan; maintain the right of the lowly and the destitute. Rescue the weak and the needy . . . Rise up, O God, judge the earth.

PRAYER—My Lord and my God, you see my heart; and my desires are not hidden from you. I am encouraged and strengthened by your goodness to me today. I want to be yours and yours alone. O my God, my Savior, my Sanctifier, hear me, help me, and show mercy to me for Jesus Christ's sake. Amen. **JW**

THURSDAY
WEEK 3 — LENTEN SEASON

PSALM 95:1-9 • JEREMIAH 7:23-28 • GALATIANS 6:1-10 • LUKE 11:14-23

MORNING MEDITATIONS

PRAYER—Our Father in heaven, hallowed be your Name, your kingdom come, your will be done, on earth as it is in heaven. Give us today our daily bread. **Forgive us our sins as we forgive those who sin against us.** Save us from the time of trial, and deliver us from evil. For the kingdom, the power, and the glory are yours, now and for ever. Amen. **BCP**

PSALM 95:6-8a—O come, let us worship and bow down, let us kneel before the Lord, our Maker! For he is our God, and we are the people of his pasture, the sheep of his hand. O that today you would listen to his voice! Do not harden your hearts.

JEREMIAH 7:23-24a *"Obey My Voice" . . . Yet They Did Not Obey*
But this command I gave them, "Obey my voice, and I will be your God, and you shall be my people; and walk only in the way that I command you, so that it may be well with you." Yet they did not obey.

GALATIANS 6:8-9a *Let Us Not Grow Weary*
If you sow to your own flesh, you will reap corruption from the flesh; but if you sow to the Spirit, you will reap eternal life from the Spirit. So let us not grow weary in doing what is right.

LUKE 11:14-23 *Today's Gospel Reading*

> In the realm of personal relationships and spiritual adjustments the philosophy of the "second mile" is particularly effective. It is amazing how quickly hard hearts are softened, strained feelings are alleviated, and misunderstandings dissolved when one persists in going the "second mile."
>
> — E. S. MANN, *THE THINGS THAT COUNT*

EVENING REFLECTIONS

PSALM 86:14-15b—You, O Lord, are a God merciful and gracious, slow to anger and abounding in steadfast love and faithfulness. Turn to me and be gracious to me; give your strength to your servant.

PRAYER—O God, let it be the one business of my life to glorify you by every thought of my heart, by every word of my tongue, by every work of my hand, and by professing your truth and love to everyone. Amen. **JW**

FRIDAY — WEEK 3, LENTEN SEASON

PSALM 81 • HOSEA 14:1-9 • GALATIANS 6:11-18 • MARK 12:28-34

MORNING MEDITATIONS

PRAYER—Our Father in heaven, hallowed be your Name, your kingdom come, your will be done, on earth as it is in heaven. Give us today our daily bread. Forgive us our sins as we forgive those who sin against us. **Save us from the time of trial, and deliver us from evil.** For the kingdom, the power, and the glory are yours, now and for ever. Amen. **BCP**

PSALM 81:8, 13—Hear, O my people, while I admonish you; O Israel, if you would but listen to me . . . O that my people would listen to me, that Israel would walk in my ways!

HOSEA 14:1, 9 *The Ways of the Lord Are Right*
Return, O Israel, to the Lord your God, for you have stumbled because of your iniquity . . . Those who are wise understand these things; those who are discerning know them. For the ways of the Lord are right, and the upright walk in them, but transgressors stumble in them.

GALATIANS 6:14 *The World Has Been Crucified to Me*
May I never boast of anything except the cross of our Lord Jesus Christ, by which the world has been crucified to me, and I to the world.

MARK 12:28-34 *Today's Gospel Reading*

> Two ways of life are open to us. One way is well traveled; the other is lonely. One way is broad and winding with a myriad of alternate routes; the other is straight and narrow. One way avoids meeting the demands of Christ; the other begins by facing eternal issues. One way leads to death; the other to life.
>
> E. S. MANN, *THE THINGS THAT COUNT*

EVENING REFLECTIONS

PSALM 92:1-2, 4a—It is good to give thanks to the Lord, to sing praises to your name, O Most High; to declare your steadfast love in the morning, and your faithfulness by night . . . For you, O Lord, have made me glad by your work.

PRAYER—Father, accept my imperfect repentance, have compassion on my infirmities, forgive my faults, purify my uncleanness, strengthen my weakness, fix my unstableness, and let your good Spirit watch over me forever, and your love ever rule in my heart, through the merits and sufferings and love of your Son, in whom you are always well pleased. Amen. **JW**

SATURDAY — WEEK 3, LENTEN SEASON

PSALM 51:1-4, 15-19 ▪ HOSEA 6:1-6 ▪ 2 JOHN 1-13 ▪ LUKE 18:9-14

MORNING MEDITATIONS

PRAYER—Our Father in heaven, hallowed be your Name, your kingdom come, your will be done, on earth as it is in heaven. Give us today our daily bread. Forgive us our sins as we forgive those who sin against us. Save us from the time of trial, and deliver us from evil. **For the kingdom, the power, and the glory are yours, now and for ever. Amen.** *BCP*

PSALM 51:1a, 17—Have mercy on me, O God, according to your steadfast love . . . The sacrifice acceptable to God is a broken spirit; a broken and contrite heart, O God, you will not despise.

HOSEA 6:1-2   *On the Third Day He Will Raise Us Up*
Come, let us return to the LORD; for it is he who has torn, and he will heal us; he has struck down, and he will bind us up. After two days he will revive us; on the third day he will raise us up, that we may live before him.

2 JOHN 6   *Walk in Love*
And this is love: that we walk according to his commandments; this is the commandment just as you have heard it from the beginning—you must walk in it.

LUKE 18:9-14   *Today's Gospel Reading*

> It is not enough that you catch a vision. The vision must capture you. It must grip you until you are moved to make a choice. Decision must follow vision. And when it does, life can be transformed; *for there is power in a right decision.*   E. S. MANN, *THE THINGS THAT COUNT*

EVENING REFLECTIONS

PSALM 90:1-2—Lord, you have been our dwelling place in all generations. Before the mountains were brought forth, or ever you had formed the earth and the world, from everlasting to everlasting you are God.

PRAYER—Thanks be to you, O Lord Jesus Christ, for all the benefits you have won for us. O merciful Redeemer, Friend, and Brother, may I know you more clearly, love you more dearly, and follow you more nearly day by day. Amen. **St. Richard of Chichester**

WEEK FOUR
Lenten Season

Sunday: Coming to Our Senses

Read the gospel passage from Luke 15:1-3, 11b-32 and the devotional reflection titled "Coming to Our Senses," then respond to the discussion prompts in the Reflective Journaling section.

THE MUSIC OF ASHES TO FIRE

Week 4: "Softly and Tenderly" (Track 5)

Monday through Saturday

IN THE MORNING:

A personal daily devotional guide includes prayer, a reading from the Old Testament, the Psalms, the Epistles, and the Gospels for each day of the week.

In addition to the daily psalm, this week's readings come from Exodus, Isaiah, Ezekiel, Jeremiah, Micah, 3 John, Jude, and the gospel of John.

Inspirational quotes from men and women of faith keep us in contact with our shared Christian heritage.

IN THE EVENING:

An evening psalm and prayer become preludes to nighttime rest and renewal.

SUNDAY

LENTEN SEASON–WEEK FOUR
Coming to Our Senses

A devotional reflection based on Luke 15:1-3, 11b-32

Read the gospel passage first, then the devotional reflection that follows. The discussion prompts at the end will help prepare you for Sunday school and small-group sessions.

Charles Dickens famously called it the greatest short story ever written. And it is indeed a great story both in its literary form and, more importantly, in its enduring meaning and impact. The message is so simple that a child can follow the story line, and yet it is profound enough to have been the subject of several book-length studies. Scholars have pored over it, line by line, for centuries.

This brief story of a father and his two sons has a penetrating appeal that touches a person's emotions and imagination. It is succinct, tightly crafted, and personally engaging. It is a narrative filled with colorful, real-life imagery. Of all the parables told by Jesus, this account of the prodigal son is the most richly detailed and most powerfully dramatic. It is a story brimming with emotion—ranging from sadness and disappointment to triumph, shock, and finally an unsettling wish for more.

This parable spreads itself across a mere twenty-some verses with so much pathos and fine detail carefully woven into its word pictures that we are drawn into it in a special way. It becomes both a mirror in which we see our image and a window through which we see God.

Yet although the story is very interesting and richly textured, the purpose is not to entertain but to instruct. One of the reasons this story touches so many is that we recognize ourselves in it. The word "parable" is transliterated from a Greek word that literally speaks of something placed alongside something else for the purpose of showing the likeness or making an association between the two things. As we lay the parable alongside our lives, we can see ourselves in a new way.

Jesus introduces the three main characters in the first sentence: "There was a man who had two sons" (Luke 15:11). And as the story unfolds, the focus shifts from one character to another, building in intensity as it goes. The younger son is the focus at the beginning, and then the father takes center stage at that magnificent moment of reconciliation. This is followed by the elder brother's response, which leaves the story hanging, somewhat unresolved.

With each movement, the plot takes a surprising turn. For example, there is the description of the boy who becomes so desperately hungry he is willing to eat husks scavenged from the slop fed to the hogs. This is an image that would have been particularly offensive to the Jews who heard the story from the lips of Jesus in the first century, and it is one that reminds us of the twenty-first century that choices have consequences. That is a lesson that too many folks only seem to learn the hard way.

Another thing that makes the tale unforgettable is the poignancy demonstrated in the father's response when his lost son returns. While the boy was still a long way off, "his father saw him and was filled with compassion" for him; "he ran" to his son, threw "his arms around him and kissed him" (v. 20). What a picture of love and grace–what a portrait of God, the Father. Who would not be moved by that kind of love and forgiveness?

The elder son is the third character to take center stage in the story, and he is not the least bit moved by his father's love. In fact, he is clearly resentful of both his brother and his father. Thus the parable of the prodigal son is not just a warm and fuzzy feel-good story but a troubling narrative as well.

There is one phrase that is particularly engaging. It is a turning point. The phrase comes after the son has taken his inheritance and gone his own way and finally lost it all. Luke 15:17 opens with these words, "But when he came to himself." Another translation says, "When he finally came to his senses" (NLT).

There needs to be a moment in our lives when we must come to ourselves, come to our senses. What does that mean? It means we see ourselves as we really are—not as we pretend to be or want to be or once were. That happens when we view our lives through the lens of Lent. In doing so, we see ourselves as the object of the Father's love and the Son's sacrifice. It is at that point that we come to our senses.

When viewed against the backdrop of Easter, the spotlight of the story of the prodigal shifts from the two sons to the father. Here we see that the love of the father can save a person not only from the indulgences of this life, as characterized by the younger son, but also from having to measure up to a life of legalism and mere moral conformity, as portrayed in the older brother.

Luke 15 reveals God as one who . . .

    searches after the one lost lamb,

        tears the house up to find a precious coin,

            and not only welcomes the son home

                but reaches out to the older brother as well.

This story casts a meaningful glance at both the death and resurrection of Jesus and the promise of eternal life as the father declares, "For this son of mine was dead and is alive again" (v. 24).

May this stop along our seasonal journey remind us that "coming to our senses" needs to be repeated from time to time as we follow Christ—and Lent is a perfect time to see ourselves anew, in the light of the loving and forgiving spirit of the Father.
        —John Bowling

After reading the passage from Luke 15:1-3, 11b-32
and the devotional reflection "Coming to Our
Senses," you may also want to read the
following related passages:

Joshua 5:9-12; Psalm 32; 2 Corinthians 5:16-21

The discussion prompts that follow will help prepare you to participate in your Sunday school class or small-group study. Use your Reflective Journaling section to record any other insights that come to you as you read the gospel lesson and the devotional reflection.

DISCUSSION PROMPT NO. 1: LUKE 15:1-3, 11b-32

In what way does Jesus' parable answer the accusation made against him, "This fellow welcomes sinners and eats with them" (v. 2)?

DISCUSSION PROMPT NO. 2: LUKE 15:1-3, 11b-32

The son who squandered his inheritance is welcomed back and restored. Why?

DISCUSSION PROMPT NO. 3: LUKE 15:1-3, 11b-32

What reasons does the older son give for his anger and refusal to celebrate his brother's return? Have you ever felt that someone did not deserve the mercy he or she received? How did you react?

DISCUSSION PROMPT NO. 4: LUKE 15:1-3, 11b-32

How does the father's reply to the elder brother show the same love and compassion extended to the younger brother?

DISCUSSION PROMPT NO. 5: DEVOTIONAL REFLECTION

Jesus says that the younger son's life began to change "When he came to himself" (v. 17). What were the circumstances in your life God used to bring you to your senses and determine in your heart to seek him?

Reflective Journaling

MONDAY — WEEK 4, LENTEN SEASON

PSALM 30:1-5, 11-12 ▪ ISAIAH 65:17-25 ▪ 3 JOHN 1-8 ▪ JOHN 4:43-54

MORNING MEDITATIONS

PRAYER—For your mercies' sake, O Lord my God, tell me what you are to me. Say to my soul: "I am your salvation." So speak that I may hear, O Lord; my heart is listening; open it that it may hear you, and say to my soul: "I am your salvation." After hearing this word, may I come to you in haste. **St. Augustine**

PSALM 30:4-5—Sing praises to the Lord, O you his faithful ones, and give thanks to his holy name. For his anger is but for a moment; his favor is for a lifetime. Weeping may linger for the night, but joy comes with the morning.

ISAIAH 65:17-18 *Be Glad and Rejoice*
For I am about to create new heavens and a new earth; the former things shall not be remembered or come to mind. But be glad and rejoice forever in what I am creating; for I am about to create Jerusalem as a joy, and its people as a delight.

3 JOHN 2a, 3-4 *Walk in the Truth*
Beloved, I pray that all may go well with you . . . I was overjoyed when some of the friends arrived and testified to your faithfulness to the truth, namely how you walk in the truth. I have no greater joy than this, to hear that my children are walking in the truth.

JOHN 4:43-54 *Today's Gospel Reading*

> The saints have exercised their senses to be self-controlled. Because they are strong in faith and understand the Word, they don't faint under trials. From time to time ever more powerful trials work against them, yet they continue to be faithful.
>
> ST. ATHANASIUS, *FESTAL LETTER 19*, PARA. 7

EVENING REFLECTIONS

PSALM 67:1-3—May God be gracious to us and bless us and make his face to shine upon us, that your way may be known upon earth, your saving power among all nations. Let the peoples praise you, O God; let all the peoples praise you.

PRAYER—Lord, make me an instrument of Thy peace. Where there is hatred, let me sow love, where there is injury, pardon; where there is doubt, faith; where there is despair hope. Amen. **The Prayer of St. Francis**

TUESDAY — WEEK 4, LENTEN SEASON

PSALM 46 ▪ EZEKIEL 47:1-9, 12 ▪ 3 JOHN 8-15 ▪ JOHN 5:1-16

MORNING MEDITATIONS

PRAYER—Lord, hide not your face from me. Let me see your face even if I die, lest I die with longing to see it. The house of my soul is too small to receive you; let it be enlarged by you. It is all in ruins; I ask you to repair it. There are things in it, I confess and know, that must offend you. From my secret sins cleanse me, O Lord, and from all others spare your servant. Amen. **St. Augustine**

PSALM 46:4-5, 10a—There is a river whose streams make glad the city of God, the holy habitation of the Most High. God is in the midst of the city; it shall not be moved; God will help it when the morning dawns . . . Be still, and know that I am God!

EZEKIEL 47:12 *Water Flows from the Sanctuary*
On the banks, on both sides of the river, there will grow all kinds of trees for food. Their leaves will not wither nor their fruit fail . . . because the water for them flows from the sanctuary. Their fruit will be for food, and their leaves for healing.

3 JOHN 11 *Imitate What Is Good*
Beloved, do not imitate what is evil but imitate what is good. Whoever does good is from God; whoever does evil has not seen God.

JOHN 5:1-16 *Today's Gospel Reading*

> This is the loving-kindness of God: He never turns his face away from a sincere repentance. God accepts and welcomes anyone who has become wicked to the greatest extreme and chooses to return towards the path of holiness.
> ST. CHRYSOSTOM, *EXHORTATION TO THEODORE AFTER HIS FALL*, 7

EVENING REFLECTIONS

PSALM 66:19-20—But truly God has listened; he has given heed to the words of my prayer. Blessed be God, because he has not rejected my prayer or removed his steadfast love from me.

PRAYER—Lord, make me an instrument of Thy peace. Where there is hatred, let me sow love . . . Where there is darkness, light; where there is sadness, joy. Amen. **The Prayer of St. Francis**

WEDNESDAY
WEEK 4 LENTEN SEASON

PSALM 145:8-20 ▪ ISAIAH 49:8-16a ▪ JUDE 1-4 ▪ JOHN 5:17-30

MORNING MEDITATIONS

PRAYER—O Lord my God, teach my heart where and how to seek you, where and how to find you. Lord, if you are not here but absent, where shall I seek you? But you are everywhere, so you must be here, therefore let me seek you. Amen. **St. Anselm of Canterbury**

PSALM 145:8-9, 20a—The LORD is gracious and merciful, slow to anger and abounding in steadfast love. The LORD is good to all, and his compassion is over all that he has made . . . The LORD watches over all who love him.

ISAIAH 49:13, 15d-16a *I Will Not Forget You*
Sing for joy, O heavens, and exult, O earth; break forth, O mountains, into singing! For the LORD has comforted his people, and will have compassion on his suffering ones . . . I will not forget you. See, I have engraved you on the palms of my hands.

JUDE 3 *Contend for the Faith*
Beloved, while eagerly preparing to write to you about the salvation we share, I find it necessary to write and appeal to you to contend for the faith that was once for all entrusted to the saints.

JOHN 5:17-30 *Today's Gospel Reading*

> He who is Lord will forgive the sins of the repentant. He will blot out all the iniquities of those who begin afresh practicing righteousness . . . Repentance makes us cautious and diligent to avoid the faults which we once were tricked into.
>
> ST. LACTANTIUS, *DIVINE INSTITUTES* 6.24

EVENING REFLECTIONS

PSALM 119:137-138, 140—You are righteous, O Lord, and your judgments are right. You have appointed your decrees in righteousness and in all faithfulness . . . Your promise is well tried, and your servant loves it.

PRAYER—Lord, make me an instrument of Thy peace; where there is hatred, let me sow love . . . O Divine Master, grant that I may not so much seek to be consoled as to console, to be understood, as to understand, to be loved, as to love. Amen. **The Prayer of St. Francis**

THURSDAY
WEEK 4 — LENTEN SEASON

PSALM 106:19-23, 47-48 ▪ EXODUS 32:7-14 ▪ JUDE 5-13 ▪ JOHN 5:31-47

MORNING MEDITATIONS

PRAYER—Lord, I am not trying to make my way to your height, for my understanding is in no way equal to that, but I do desire to understand a little of your truth which my heart already believes and loves. I do not seek to understand so that I may believe, but I believe so that I may understand; and what is more, I believe that unless I do believe I shall not understand. **St. Anselm of Canterbury**

PSALM 106:21, 23, 47a—They forgot God, their Savior, who had done great things in Egypt . . . Therefore he said he would destroy them—had not Moses . . . stood in the breach before him, to turn away his wrath from destroying them . . . Save us, O LORD our God.

EXODUS 32:11, 12b-13a *O Lord, Change Your Mind*
Moses implored the LORD his God, and said, "O LORD, why does your wrath burn hot against your people, whom you brought out of the land of Egypt . . . ? Turn from your fierce wrath; change your mind and do not bring disaster on your people. Remember Abraham, Isaac, and Israel, your servants."

JUDE 5 *The Lord Saved a People Out of Egypt*
Now I desire to remind you, though you are fully informed, that the Lord, who once for all saved a people out of the land of Egypt, afterward destroyed those who did not believe.

JOHN 5:31-47 *Today's Gospel Reading*

> Depart from that wicked spirit of anger and put on patience. Resist anger and bitterness, and you will be found in company with the purity that is loved by the Lord.
> SHEPHERD OF HERMAS, *COMMANDMENTS* 5.2

EVENING REFLECTIONS

PSALM 19:12b, 14—Clear me from hidden faults . . . Let the words of my mouth and the meditation of my heart be acceptable to you, O LORD, my rock and my redeemer.

PRAYER—Lord, make me an instrument of Thy peace; where there is hatred, let me sow love . . . For it is in giving, that we receive, it is in pardoning, that we are pardoned, it is in dying, that we are born to eternal life. **The Prayer of St. Francis**

FRIDAY | WEEK 4 LENTEN SEASON

PSALM 34:15-22 ▪ MICAH 6:6-8 ▪ JUDE 14-19 ▪ JOHN 7:1-2, 10, 25-30

MORNING MEDITATIONS

PRAYER—O God, the author of peace and lover of concord, to know you is eternal life, to serve you is perfect freedom: defend us your servants from all assaults of our enemies, that we may trust in your defense and not fear the power of any adversaries; through Jesus Christ our Lord. **Celtic prayer**

PSALM 34:17-18—When the righteous cry for help, the Lord hears, and rescues them from all their troubles. The Lord is near to the brokenhearted, and saves the crushed in spirit.

MICAH 6:8 *Do Justice, Love Kindness*
He has told you, O mortal, what is good; and what does the Lord require of you but to do justice, and to love kindness, and to walk humbly with your God?

JUDE 14b-15 *The Lord Is Coming*
The Lord is coming with ten thousands of his holy ones, to execute judgment on all, and to convict everyone of all the deeds of ungodliness that they have committed.

JOHN 7:1-2, 10, 25-30 *Today's Gospel Reading*

> God works in us so that we can have the will to obey. Once we have this will, God works with us to perfect us. The apostle Paul says, "I am confident of this very thing, that he which hath begun a good work in you will perform it until the day of Jesus Christ."
>
> ST. AUGUSTINE, *ON GRACE AND FREE WILL* 33

EVENING REFLECTIONS

PSALM 107:1, 42-43—O give thanks to the Lord, for he is good; for his steadfast love endures forever . . . The upright see it and are glad; and all wickedness stops its mouth. Let those who are wise give heed to these things, and consider the steadfast love of the Lord.

PRAYER—Father, strengthen the hearts of your church and all your servants. Give us grace to consecrate ourselves faithfully and entirely to your service. Help us to encourage one another in love and grow together as your people, through the merits of Our Lord and Savior Jesus Christ. Amen. **JW**

SATURDAY | WEEK 4 LENTEN SEASON

PSALM 7:1-2, 9-11, 17 ▪ **JEREMIAH 10:1-10** ▪ **JUDE 20-25** ▪ **JOHN 7:40-53**

MORNING MEDITATIONS

PRAYER—God be in my head, and in my understanding; God be in mine eyes, and in my looking; God be in my mouth, and in my speaking; God be in my heart, and in my thinking; God be at mine end, and at my departing. Through Christ, my Lord, I pray. Amen. **Celtic prayer**

PSALM 7:10-11a, 17—God is my shield, who saves the upright in heart. God is a righteous judge . . . I will give to the Lord the thanks due to his righteousness, and sing praise to the name of the Lord, the Most High.

JEREMIAH 10:6-7   *The Lord Is the True God*
There is none like you, O Lord; you are great, and your name is great in might. Who would not fear you, O King of the nations? For that is your due; among all the wise ones of the nations and in all their kingdoms there is no one like you.

JUDE 20-21   *Look Forward to the Mercy of Our Lord Jesus Christ*
But you, beloved, build yourselves up on your most holy faith; pray in the Holy Spirit; keep yourselves in the love of God; look forward to the mercy of our Lord Jesus Christ that leads to eternal life.

JOHN 7:40-53   *Today's Gospel Reading*

> I bind unto myself today—the power of God to hold and lead, his eye to watch, his might to stay, his ear to hearken to my need. The wisdom of my God to teach, his hand to guide, his shield to ward, the word of God to give me speech, his heavenly host to be my guard.
> *FROM ST. PATRICK'S BREASTPLATE*

EVENING REFLECTIONS

PSALM 33:20-22—Our soul waits for the Lord; he is our help and shield. Our heart is glad in him, because we trust in his holy name. Let your steadfast love, O Lord, be upon us, even as we hope in you.

PRAYER—Be present, O merciful God, and protect us through the silent hours of this night, so that we who are wearied by the changes and chances of this fleeting world may repose upon your eternal changelessness; through Jesus Christ our Lord. Amen. **Gelasian Sacramentary**

WEEK FIVE
*L*ENTEN *S*EASON

Sunday: And the Fragrance Filled the House

Read the gospel passage from John 12:1-8 and the devotional
reflection titled "And the Fragrance Filled the House,"
then respond to the discussion prompts
in the Reflective Journaling section.

THE MUSIC OF ASHES TO FIRE

Week 5: "Fill This House" (Track 6)

Monday through Saturday

IN THE MORNING:

A personal daily devotional guide includes prayer,
a reading from the Old Testament, the Psalms, the Epistles,
and the Gospels for each day of the week.

In addition to the daily psalm, this week's readings come
from Genesis, Numbers, Ezekiel, Daniel, Jeremiah,
Hebrews, and the gospel of John.

Inspirational quotes from men and women of faith keep
us in contact with our shared Christian heritage.

IN THE EVENING:

An evening psalm and prayer become preludes
to nighttime rest and renewal.

LENTEN SEASON—WEEK FIVE
And the Fragrance Filled the House

A devotional reflection based on John 12:1-8

Read the gospel passage first, then the devotional reflection that follows. The discussion prompts at the end will help prepare you for Sunday school and small-group sessions.

The story is told of a village in the south of France where many of the townsfolk worked in a small factory that produced lavender perfume. In the late afternoon, when the whistle blew signaling the end of the workday, each worker would gather his or her personal belongings and begin walking home through the village, stopping at shops, markets, or cafés. Each evening then, little by little, through the presence of these workers, the entire village was scented with the sweet fragrance of lavender that lingered on the workers' clothing.

Similarly, there is an intriguing and multilayered story from John's gospel telling of a house filled not only with the fragrance of an expensive perfume but also with the essence of an extravagant love. John 12:1-8 relates a story filled with character sketches: Martha serving, Lazarus reclining, Judas scheming, Jews observing, and Mary carrying out a very personal but startling expression of love and devotion. "Mary took a pound of costly perfume made of pure nard, anointed Jesus' feet, and wiped them with her hair. The house was filled with the fragrance of the perfume" (v. 3).

The gospel of John is divided into two major sections. The first twelve chapters relate the public ministry of Jesus among the people in general. The second half of the gospel, chapters 13—21, focuses on the last week of Jesus' life, recounting the farewell dialogues of Jesus as he prepares his disciples for his death and detailing his resurrection and subsequent appearances.

Since the story of Mary's anointing of Jesus is near the end of the first section in John's gospel, it occupies a pivotal point. This act on the part of Mary is the hinge on which the passage turns. It is the final event depicted before Jesus enters Jerusalem for the last time, on the day we now call Palm Sunday. John 12:1-8 provides a link between what has happened and what will happen.

It was customary in the homes of that day for the host to have the servants wash the feet of guests. Mary's actions, however, take this common practice to an entirely new level.

- First, Mary performs the foot washing; *she* becomes the servant. She bears public witness to her devotion to Christ.
- Second, a woman normally would never touch a man except for her husband or sons—and then only in private. Her commitment to Jesus overshadows all the constraints of custom.
- Third, a woman would never allow anyone other than her immediate family to see her hair. Thus this would be an act of unpretentiousness as well as devotion.
- Fourth, here the washing of the feet was done not with water but with expensive, fragrant perfume—costing a full year's wages, according to Judas. Mary gives her best as Jesus' death draws near.
- Fifth, this was an atypical anointing. Per the customs of the day, anointing took place in one of two ways: by placing oil on the *head* of an individual being installed as a priest, prophet, or king or by anointing the *entire body*, as was done for the dead.

So why anoint the feet? What did the act signify?

Here is a moment when humility and service reveal a glimpse of the kingdom. Before many days, Jesus will wash the feet of his disciples saying,

Do you know what I have done to you? You call me Teacher and Lord—and you are right, for that is what I am. So if I, your Lord and Teacher, have washed your feet, you also ought to wash one another's feet. For I have set you an example, that you also should do as I have done to you. Very truly, I tell you, servants are not greater than their master, nor are messengers greater than the one who sent them. If you know these things, you are blessed if you do them. (13:12b-17)

Rather than waiting until after his death, Mary expresses her love, devotion, and sacrifice while Jesus is still with them. By anointing Jesus now Mary is giving the very best she has to the living Jesus as an outpouring of her love. Judas protests the "waste." Yet the real waste would have been to devote her effort and her expensive gift to the dead. Rather than give what she has in memoriam, she gives it in witness to the living presence of Christ.

Several years ago, when my father was terminally ill, I sat at the foot of his bed many days, often massaging his feet and, yes, even using fragrant oil, seeking to express something words could not convey. Possibly this was similar to the actions of Mary, who perhaps was sensing the immanent death of Jesus.

Mary's devotion gives evidence that love is not love if it counts the cost—love gives its all. This story is filled with giving. Martha is giving—she makes and serves the dinner. Lazarus gives his witness by showing himself to the guests as proof of Jesus' power. Mary gives a very expensive, sacrificial gift. All of that is set against the backdrop of John's gospel, which so eloquently reduces the whole gospel to a single sentence that begins with the words, "For God so loved . . . he gave" (3:16a). —Jill Bowling

After reading the passage from John 12:1-8 and the devotional reflection "And the Fragrance Filled the House," you may also want to read the following related passages:
Isaiah 43:16-21; Psalm 126; and Philippians 3:4b-14

The discussion prompts that follow will help prepare you to participate in your Sunday school class or small-group study. Use your Reflective Journaling section to record any other insights that come to you as you read the gospel lesson and the devotional reflection.

DISCUSSION PROMPT NO. 1: JOHN 12:1-8
John tells us that Mary "took a pound of costly perfume made of pure nard" (v. 3) and poured it on Jesus' feet. Have you ever felt moved to give a lavish gift to God? When and why?

DISCUSSION PROMPT NO. 2: JOHN 12:1-8
The fragrance of Mary's gift filled the house where Jesus and his disciples were dinner guests. How can a generous gift change the atmosphere in a group or situation?

DISCUSSION PROMPT NO. 3: JOHN 12:1-8

Judas objected to what he considered the "waste" of this expensive perfume. John tells us he was a thief and did not really care for the poor. How easy can it be to use a practical objection to cover a dishonorable motive?

DISCUSSION PROMPT NO. 4: JOHN 12:1-8

Jesus' response indicated that he had a very different interpretation of Mary's actions than did Judas. In what ways did Jesus view her gift differently?

DISCUSSION PROMPT NO. 5: DEVOTIONAL REFLECTION

Mary provides an example of humble service. Jesus later duplicates this example when he washes the disciples' feet (John 13). What examples of humble service have you seen? What did these examples inspire you to do?

Reflective Journaling

MONDAY | WEEK 5 LENTEN SEASON

PSALM 17:1-8, 15 ▪ EZEKIEL 36:16-38 ▪ HEBREWS 10:1-18 ▪ JOHN 11:1-45

MORNING MEDITATIONS

PRAYER—Almighty God, you alone can bring into order all the unruly affections of my life. I pray that you will give me grace to love what you command and desire what you promise so that my heart may be focused where true joy is found. In the name and for the sake of Jesus Christ, I pray. Amen. **JW**

PSALM 17:3ab, 5, 7a—If you try my heart, if you visit me by night, if you test me, you will find no wickedness in me . . . My steps have held fast to your paths; my feet have not slipped . . . Wondrously show your steadfast love, O savior of those who seek refuge.

EZEKIEL 36:26-27   *A New Heart*
A new heart I will give you, and a new spirit I will put within you; and I will remove from your body the heart of stone and give you a heart of flesh. I will put my spirit within you, and make you follow my statutes.

HEBREWS 10:15, 16b-17   *I Will Put My Laws in Their Hearts*
And the Holy Spirit also testifies to us, for after saying, ". . . I will put my laws in their hearts, and I will write them on their minds," he also adds, "I will remember their sins and their lawless deeds no more."

JOHN 11:1-45   *Today's Gospel Reading*

> In Christ, the one and only God has come. It is a confession of faith which I am constrained and bound to make, because the more I confront myself with the fact of Christ, the more intensely do I know that the living God is confronting me demanding the entire and utter surrender of my soul.
> — JAMES STEWART, *THE STRONG NAME*

EVENING REFLECTIONS

PSALM 145:13b-14, 21—The Lord is faithful in all his words, and gracious in all his deeds. The Lord upholds all who are falling, and raises up all who are bowed down . . . My mouth will speak the praise of the Lord, and . . . bless his holy name forever and ever.

PRAYER—Teach me, O Lord, to go through all of my activities with a truly devoted heart, so that I may see you in all things, and know that you are continually aware of me. Search my motives so that I may never weaken the liberty of spirit which is so necessary for the love of you. Amen. **JW**

TUESDAY — WEEK 5, LENTEN SEASON

PSALM 102:1-2, 16-21 • NUMBERS 21:4-9 • HEBREWS 10:19-31 • JOHN 8:21-30

MORNING MEDITATIONS

PRAYER—Father in Heaven! You have loved us first. Grant that this conviction might discipline my soul so that my heart might remain faithful and sincere in the love which I owe to all those whom you have commanded me to love as I love myself. Amen. **Søren Kierkegaard**

PSALM 102:18a, 19a, 20b—Let this be recorded for a generation to come . . . that [the Lord] looked down from his holy height . . . to set free those who were doomed to die.

NUMBERS 21:8-9 *Look and Live*
The Lord said to Moses, "Make a poisonous serpent, and set it on a pole; and everyone who is bitten shall look at it and live." So Moses made a serpent of bronze, and put it upon a pole; and whenever a serpent bit someone, that person would look at the serpent of bronze and live.

HEBREWS 10:19-22a *We Have a Great Priest*
Therefore, my friends, since we have confidence to enter the sanctuary by the blood of Jesus, by the new and living way that he opened for us through the curtain (that is, through his flesh), and since we have a great priest over the house of God, let us approach with a true heart in full assurance faith.

JOHN 8:21-30 *Today's Gospel Reading*

> You begin exploring the fact of Christ, perhaps merely intellectually and theologically—and before you know where you are, the fact is exploring you, spiritually and morally . . . You set out to see what you can find in Christ, and sooner or later God in Christ finds you.
>
> JAMES STEWART, *THE STRONG NAME*

EVENING REFLECTIONS

PSALM 35:9-10a, 18—My soul shall rejoice in the Lord, exulting in his deliverance . . . O Lord, who is like you? . . . I will thank you in the great congregation; in the mighty throng I will praise you.

PRAYER—Almighty God, your love for us is more than we could ever imagine. Fill our lives with your love, our minds with your thoughts, our mouths with your truth, so that every part of our living is touched by your grace. Amen.

WEDNESDAY
WEEK 5 LENTEN SEASON

PSALM 18:46-50 ▪ DANIEL 3:13-20, 24-28 ▪ HEBREWS 11:1-7 ▪ JOHN 8:31-42

MORNING MEDITATIONS

PRAYER—O God, fill me with confidence and trust that in knowing your will, I may follow it, and that in following your will, I will find joy, through Jesus Christ, my Lord. Amen.

PSALM 18:46, 48-49—The Lord lives! Blessed be my rock, and exalted be the God of my salvation . . . who delivered me from my enemies; indeed, you exalted me above my adversaries; you delivered me from the violent. For this I will extol you, O Lord . . . and sing praises to your name.

DANIEL 3:28 *He Sent His Angel and Delivered His Servants*
Nebuchadnezzar said, "Blessed be the God of Shadrach, Meshach, and Abednego, who has sent his angel and delivered his servants . . . They disobeyed the king's command and yielded up their bodies rather than . . . worship any god except their own God."

HEBREWS 11:6 *God Rewards Those Who Seek Him*
And without faith it is impossible to please God, for whoever would approach him must believe that he exists and that he rewards those who diligently seek him.

JOHN 8:31-42 *Today's Gospel Reading*

> It is the saintliest people in the world who have been most conscious of their own sin. Read the stories of the saints, the spiritual history of a Paul, a Thomas à Kempis, a Teresa, and in every case this fact confronts you—that in proportion as a soul draws close to God, the more vividly does it realize its own personal unworthiness.
>
> JAMES STEWART, *THE STRONG NAME*

EVENING REFLECTIONS

PSALM 128:1-2, 4—Happy is everyone who fears the Lord, who walks in his ways. You shall eat the fruit of the labor of your hands; you shall be happy, and it shall go well with you . . . Thus shall [the one] be blessed who fears the Lord.

PRAYER—Almighty God, in whom we live and move and have our being, you have made us for yourself, and our hearts are restless till they find their rest in you. Grant us such purity of heart and strength of purpose that no selfish passion may hinder us from knowing your will, and no weakness from doing it; but that in your light we may see light, and in your service find perfect freedom, through Jesus Christ our Lord. **St. Augustine**

THURSDAY
WEEK 5 — LENTEN SEASON

PSALM 105:1-11 ▪ GENESIS 17:1-9 ▪ HEBREWS 11:8-22 ▪ JOHN 8:51-59

MORNING MEDITATIONS

PRAYER—Father in Heaven! You have loved us first; help me never to forget that you are love, so that this sure conviction might triumph in my heart over the seduction of the world, over the anxiety for the future, over the fright of the past, over the distress of the moment. Amen. *Søren Kierkegaard*

PSALM 105:4-6—Seek the LORD and his strength; seek his presence continually. Remember the wonderful works he has done, his miracles, and the judgments he has uttered, O offspring of his servant Abraham, children of Jacob, his chosen ones.

GENESIS 17:1, 7ab   *Walk Before Me and Be Blameless*
When Abram was ninety-nine years old, the LORD appeared to Abram, and said to him, "I am God Almighty; walk before me, and be blameless . . . I will establish my covenant between me and you, and your offspring after you throughout the generations."

HEBREWS 11:17, 19   *He Was Ready to Offer Up His Only Son*
By faith Abraham, when put to the test, offered up Isaac. He who had received the promises was ready to offer up his only son . . . He considered the fact that God is able even to raise someone from the dead—and figuratively speaking, he did receive him back.

JOHN 8:51-59   *Today's Gospel Reading*

> Think of other great religious teachers—Socrates, Buddha, Confucius—then ask, What was their paramount concern? Not to fix attention upon themselves, but to win acceptance for their message . . . But with Jesus and with him alone it is utterly different. He deliberately places himself at the very center of his own message. His supreme concern is not to implant some abstract truth in his hearer's mind; it is to win their devotion to his own person.
>
> JAMES STEWART, *THE STRONG NAME*

EVENING REFLECTIONS

PSALM 142:1-3—With my voice I cry to the LORD; with my voice I make supplication to the LORD. I pour out my complaint before him; I tell my trouble before him. When my spirit is faint, you know my way.

PRAYER—Father, grant me forgiveness of what is past, that in the days to come I may with a pure spirit, do your will—walking humbly with you, showing love to all, and keeping body and soul in sanctification and honor, in Jesus' name. Amen. *JW*

FRIDAY — WEEK 5, LENTEN SEASON

PSALM 18:1-7 • JEREMIAH 20:10-13 • HEBREWS 11:23-40 • JOHN 10:31-42

MORNING MEDITATIONS

PRAYER—O God, fill my soul with so entire a love for you, that I may love nothing but you. Give me grace to study your knowledge daily, that the more I know you, the more I may love you, through Jesus Christ my Lord. Amen. **JW**

PSALM 18:3, 6acd—I call upon the Lord, who is worthy to be praised, so I shall be saved from my enemies . . . In my distress I called upon the Lord . . . from his temple he heard my voice, and my cry to him reached his ears.

JEREMIAH 20:12-13 *You Test the Righteous*
O Lord of hosts, you test the righteous, you see the heart and the mind; let me see your retribution upon them, for to you I have committed my cause. Sing to the Lord; praise the Lord! For he has delivered the life of the needy from the hands of evildoers.

HEBREWS 11:32-34 *What Shall I More Say?*
And what should I more say? For time would fail me to tell of Gideon, Barak, Samson, Jephthah, of David and Samuel and the prophets—who through faith conquered kingdoms, administered justice, obtained promises, shut the mouths of lions, quenched raging fire, escaped the edge of the sword, won strength out of weakness, became mighty in war, put foreign armies to flight.

JOHN 10:31-42 *Today's Gospel Reading*

> Because the promise of God that, from mortality and corruption, from this weak and abject state, from dust and ashes, we could become equal to the angels of God seemed incredible to men, he not only made a written covenant . . . but also gave them a Mediator as a pledge of his promise.
>
> — ST. AUGUSTINE, *DISCOURSES ON THE PSALMS*

EVENING REFLECTIONS

PSALM 143:9-10—Save me, O Lord, from my enemies; I have fled to you for refuge. Teach me to do your will, for you are my God. Let your good spirit lead me on a level path.

PRAYER—O my Father, my God, I ask you to deliver me from any passion that obstructs my knowledge and love of you. Let none of them find a way into my heart, but instead give me a meek and gentle spirit. Reign in my heart; may I always be your servant and love you entirely, through Christ I pray. Amen. **JW**

SATURDAY
WEEK 5 LENTEN SEASON

PSALM 18:8-19 • EZEKIEL 37:21-28 • HEBREWS 12:1-2, 14-29 • JOHN 11:45-56

MORNING MEDITATIONS

PRAYER—O Lord, I know that you have commanded me, and therefore it is my duty, to love you with all my heart, and with all my strength. I know you are infinitely holy and overflowing in all perfection, and therefore it is my duty to love you. Yet not only my duty, but my joy, in Jesus' name. Amen. **JW**

PSALM 18:12-13, 16, 19—Out of the brightness before him there broke through his clouds hailstones and coals of fire. The LORD also thundered in the heavens, and the Most High uttered his voice . . . He reached down from on high . . . he drew me out of mighty waters. He brought me out into a broad place; he delivered me, because he delighted in me.

EZEKIEL 37:26-27 *I Will Be Their God*
I will make a covenant of peace with them; it shall be an everlasting covenant with them; and I will bless them and multiply them, and will set my sanctuary among them forevermore . . . I will be their God, and they shall be my people.

HEBREWS 12:14, 28-29 *Our God Is a Consuming Fire*
Pursue peace with everyone, and the holiness without which no one will see the Lord . . . Since we are receiving a kingdom that cannot be shaken, let us give thanks, by which we offer to God an acceptable worship . . . for indeed our God is a consuming fire.

JOHN 11:45-56 *Today's Gospel Reading*

> Come, come, let us go up together to the Mount of Olives. Together, let us meet Christ, who is returning from Bethany and going of his own accord . . . to complete the mystery of our salvation. And so he comes, willingly taking the road to Jerusalem, he who came down from the heights for us, to raise us who lie in the depths to exaltation with him.
>
> ST. ANDREW OF CRETE

EVENING REFLECTIONS

PSALM 43:5—Why are you cast down, O my soul, and why are you disquieted within me? Hope in God; for I shall again praise him, my help and my God.

PRAYER—O Eternal God, my Savior and Lord, I acknowledge that all I am and all I have is yours. I pray that you will surround me with such a sense of your infinite goodness, that I may return to you all possible love and obedience, through Jesus Christ, Amen. **JW**

WEEK SIX (HOLY WEEK)
Lenten Season

Sunday: Praise Is God's Alone

Read the gospel passage from Luke 19:28-40 and the
devotional reflection titled "Praise Is God's Alone,"
then respond to the discussion prompts
in the Reflective Journaling section.

THE MUSIC OF ASHES TO FIRE

Week 6: "All Creatures of Our God and King" (Track 7)

Monday through Saturday

IN THE MORNING:

A personal daily devotional guide includes prayer,
a reading from the Old Testament, the Psalms, the Epistles,
and the Gospels for each day of the week.

In addition to the daily psalm, this week's readings come from
Isaiah, Genesis, Philippians, 1 Corinthians, 1 Peter, Hebrews,
and the gospels of Matthew, Luke, and John.

Inspirational quotes from men and women of faith keep
us in contact with our shared Christian heritage.

IN THE EVENING:

An evening psalm and prayer become preludes
to nighttime rest and renewal.

PALM SUNDAY

Lenten Season—Week Six
Praise Is God's Alone

A devotional reflection based on Luke 19:28-40

Read the gospel passage first, then the devotional reflection that follows. The discussion prompts at the end will help prepare you for Sunday school and small-group sessions.

I couldn't believe my eyes, but the pounding of my heart was telling me the truth. It was actually the president of the United States, Ronald Reagan, standing just several yards in front of me. Like the many people around me, I was utterly astounded by the long, black limousines, the dark suits and shiny shoes, and the crowd members struggling for a better view. I was completely enthralled with the Secret Service men that mysteriously spoke into their hands and strangely kept touching their ears. The crowd's loud and repeated chant, "Four more years! Four more years! Four more years!" rang in my ears. As my father tightened his grip on my hand to keep from losing me in the swarm of people, I noticed the excitement of the crowd increasing. Everyone was expressing their esteem for the president by shouting joyfully and expectantly at the top of their lungs.

There were few naysayers in this crowd. Most of the people were just like my father, wanting to support the efforts of a man who promised his country, above all else, *possibility*. I don't remember being there for Republican or Democratic reasons. I do, however, remember being there for wholly civil reasons. My father and the many others in attendance were gathered on Ty Cobb Field in Endicott, New York, for one reason—the *possibility* of a different way forward. Either President Reagan was going to bring more jobs, a stronger defense structure, lower taxes, an increase in consumerism for small businesses, a war on drugs, a stronger commitment to social security, and a better overall way of life for all New Yorkers, or the people's hopes would be crushed.

Having been mesmerized by all the parade-like surroundings, I don't recall much of the president's speech that day. I do remember the president saying, "Opportunity, the chance to work hard and make our dreams come true—this is just what our administration is laboring to provide."* The possibility of a better way forward for everyone was the promise, and the thousands of people who gathered for that rally believed that Reagan would deliver.

When I read Luke 19:28-40, I am thrust back in time to 1984. I was just eleven when I saw the president, but you don't forget an experience like that. In the same way, I won't forget a passage like this one. The people in these verses, like those at the Reagan rally, were holding on to the hope that this Jesus might be the Messiah, the One to deliver them from the Romans. Could this be the One who would make the impossible possible?

Certainly Jerusalem had seen its fair share of grand entrances over the years. Kings, military leaders, and others had all ridden donkeys accompanied by brilliant complementary regimes. But Jerusalem had never seen a king quite like Jesus. Jesus came alone, accompanied only by his mission. He came into Jerusalem in peace, not to conquer or declare victory through the use of violence. Jesus spoke of a kingdom that was upside down. Jesus' kingdom didn't make sense. Jesus taught and commanded his disciples to value the least in society, the very people Roman corruption and luxury was built on. Jesus provided a way for the ordinary fisherman and tax collector, as well as for the beggar, the blind, the demon possessed, and the crippled, to find hope or to dream the impossible was possible.

Let's be honest, the clothing thrown down in front of the donkey on which Jesus was riding was not regal. Those garments were likely tattered and faded (v. 35). The hems were probably loose, and the quality poor even when new. The people who followed Jesus weren't the elite; they were the erased. No one counted many of the followers of Jesus as citizens. The people who followed Jesus, the King, were assured of only one thing—prospect. The government had already written these people off, and the citizens of the Roman Empire had done the same. It was on this man called Jesus that their hopes were based (and ultimately ruined [see Luke 24:21]).

The crowd members depicted in the Scriptures at that hopeful moment of the triumphal entry were shouting for joy, and they had good reason to

---

*http://www.reagan.utexas.edu/archives/speeches/1984/91284f.htm.

WEEK 6 ▪ LENTEN SEASON

shout—for they were well aware of Jesus' ministry throughout the region of Galilee. I'm sure that many of those in the crowd had directly or indirectly experienced the healing miracles of Jesus. Each person there who shouted, even above the skepticism and condemnation of the Pharisees (19:39), shouted with eager anticipation for what he or she yearned—liberation.

We know now, on the other side of this hopeful moment, what the people in the crowd didn't know. That is, we know and experience the liberation Jesus would bring as King, just not the kind of liberation Israel had expected. Even the rocks would have to cry out (v. 40) about this soon-to-be-realized deliverance if the crowd had not. Jesus was King, and there was nothing at that moment left undone about that declaration except the missional act of the crucifixion.

Our lives are filled with dashed hopes. Life never seems to work out quite the way we wish. But just as Jesus is a different kind of king with a different kind of kingdom, God's ways are often extraordinary. They are mighty and magnificent at the same time. However, they are certainly never predictable. If they are promised to us, they will prevail. That doesn't mean, however, that we always fully understand God's ways.

We have freedom from sin and despair because of this different kind of King who rules a different kind of kingdom. We have hope in our King, Jesus. This hope is that each and every day, all creation is being redeemed. The redemptive activity of God is something for us to excitedly engage in. Our freedom from sin and despair produces communities of people that are inspired by God's promises of possibility. These promises direct us to shout, "Blessed is the king who comes in the name of the Lord! Peace in heaven, and glory in the highest heaven!" (v. 38). We all ought to cheer loudly with our daily words and deeds in the procession of Jesus! We all ought to throw our garments down, living expectantly with the hope that one day all creation will be made new through the saving work of Jesus, our King. We place our hope in God alone, not in humanity, nor in the human will. Praise is God's alone. —Chris Folmsbee

**After reading the passage from Luke 19:28-40
and the devotional reflection "Praise Is God's Alone,"
you may also want to read the following
related passages:**

Isaiah 50:4-9a; Psalm 31:9-16; Philippians 2:5-11

The discussion prompts that follow will help prepare you to participate in your Sunday school class or small-group study. Use your Reflective Journaling section to record any other insights that come to you as you read the gospel lesson and the devotional reflection.

DISCUSSION PROMPT NO. 1: LUKE 19:28-40
Jesus has his disciples borrow a donkey for his entrance into Jerusalem. They were to tell anyone who asked, "The Lord needs it" (v. 34). Has God ever asked for anything in your life? What was your response?

DISCUSSION PROMPT NO. 2: LUKE 19:28-40
The disciples and the crowd began "to praise God . . . for all the deeds of power that they had seen" (v. 37). What is it that moves your heart to praise God?

DISCUSSION PROMPT NO. 3: LUKE 19:28-40
What does it mean to proclaim Jesus "the king who comes in the name of the Lord" (v. 38a)? In what way does he bring "peace in heaven, and glory in the highest" (v. 38b)?

DISCUSSION PROMPT NO. 4: LUKE 19:41-44
Rather than being enthralled with the praise of the crowd, Jesus wept as he looked over the city (see v. 41). Why would sorrow come to Jerusalem? Why would people not recognize "the time of [their] visitation from God" (v. 44)?

DISCUSSION PROMPT NO. 5: DEVOTIONAL REFLECTION
The crowd proclaimed Jesus as King with loud voices and by spreading their cloaks on the road before him. In what ways do you express that Jesus is King in your life? How is Jesus a different kind of king who rules a different kind of kingdom?

REFLECTIVE JOURNALING

_____
_____
_____
_____

MONDAY
WEEK 6 † HOLY WEEK / LENTEN SEASON

PSALM 27:1-3, 13-14 ▪ ISAIAH 42:1-9 ▪ PHILIPPIANS 3:1-11 ▪ JOHN 12:1-11

MORNING MEDITATIONS

PRAYER—O God, let me live this whole day for the purpose for which it was intended—in works of mercy and necessity; in prayer, praise and meditation; and let the words of my mouth and the meditation of my heart be always acceptable in your sight. Amen. **JW**

PSALM 27:1, 13-14—The Lord is my light and my salvation; whom shall I fear? The Lord is the stronghold of my life, of whom shall I be afraid? . . . I believe I shall see the goodness of the Lord in the land of the living. Wait for the Lord; be strong, and let your heart take courage.

ISAIAH 42:6c-8a *A Light to the Nations*
I have given you as a covenant to the people, a light to the nations, to open the eyes that are blind, to bring out the prisoners from the dungeon, from the prison those who sit in darkness. I am the Lord, that is my name; my glory I give to no other.

PHILIPPIANS 3:10-11 *Sharing in His Sufferings*
I want to know Christ and the power of his resurrection and the sharing of his sufferings by becoming like him in his death, if somehow I may attain the resurrection from the dead.

JOHN 12:1-11 *Today's Gospel Reading*

> Choose life—choose God! Choosing God means, according to Deuteronomy, loving him, entering into a fellowship of mind and heart with him, trusting him, entrusting oneself *to* him, and walking in his ways.
> JOSEPH RATZINGER, *ON THE WAY TO JESUS CHRIST*

EVENING REFLECTIONS

PSALM 69:16-18—Answer me, O Lord, for your steadfast love is good; according to your abundant mercy, turn to me. Do not hide your face from your servant, for I am in distress—make haste to answer me. Draw near to me, redeem me, set me free because of my enemies.

PRAYER—Christ be with me, Christ within me, Christ behind me, Christ before me, Christ beside me, Christ to win me, Christ to comfort and restore me. Christ beneath me, Christ above me, Christ in quiet, Christ in danger, Christ in hearts of all who love me, Christ in mouth of friend and stranger. **St. Patrick's Breastplate**

TUESDAY
WEEK 6 † HOLY WEEK
LENTEN SEASON

PSALM 71:1-6, 15, 17 ▪ ISAIAH 49:1-6 ▪ PHILIPPIANS 3:12—4:1 ▪ JOHN 13:21-38

MORNING MEDITATIONS

PRAYER—Eternal and Merciful Father, I know you have created me, and that I have neither being nor blessing but what is the effect of your power and goodness. I know that you are the end for which I was created, and that I can expect no happiness but in you. So, I bless your name. Amen. **JW**

PSALM 71:3, 5, 6c—Be to me a rock of refuge, a strong fortress, to save me . . . For you, O Lord, are my hope, my trust, O LORD, from my youth . . . My praise is continually of you.

ISAIAH 49:6 *Salvation to the End of the Earth*
It is too light a thing that you should be my servant to raise up the tribes of Jacob and to restore the survivors of Israel; I will give you as a light to the nations, that my salvation may reach to the end of the earth.

PHILIPPIANS 3:13b-14 *I Press On*
This one thing I do: forgetting what lies behind and straining forward to what lies ahead, I press on toward the goal for the prize of the heavenly call of God in Christ Jesus.

JOHN 13:21-33, 36-38 *Today's Gospel Reading*

> The lightning flash of God which pierces the defenses of our blindness and sin is the light of redeeming love. All this is focused at the cross. All the powers of God, on the one hand to desolate the soul with shame, on the other to kindle it with joy unspeakable and full of glory, are concentrated there. — JAMES STEWART, *THE STRONG NAME*

EVENING REFLECTIONS

PSALM 94:16-17, 22—Who rises up for me against the wicked? Who stands for me against evildoers? If the LORD had not been my help, my soul would soon have lived in the land of silence . . . But the LORD has become my stronghold, and my God the rock of my refuge.

PRAYER—O Christ Jesus, when all is darkness and I feel my weakness and helplessness, give me the sense of your presence, your love, and your strength. Help me to have perfect trust in your protecting love and strengthening power, so that nothing may frighten or worry us; for in living close to you I shall see your hand, your purpose, your will through all things.
St. Ignatius of Loyola

WEDNESDAY
WEEK 6 † HOLY WEEK
LENTEN SEASON

PSALM 69:6-8, 19-33 ▪ ISAIAH 50:4-9a ▪ PHILIPPIANS 4:1-20 ▪ MATTHEW 26:14-25

MORNING MEDITATIONS

PRAYER—My Lord and my God, let it be the one desire of my heart to live as my Master lived, whose whole life declared, "Father, not my will but your will be done." Give me grace today to follow his pattern and to walk in his steps. Give me grace to take up my cross daily and bear any hardship for his sake. Amen. **JW**

PSALM 69:20-21, 29—Insults have broken my heart, so that I am in despair. I looked for pity, but there was none; and for comforters, but I found none. They gave me poison for food, and for my thirst they gave me vinegar to drink . . . I am lowly and in pain; let your salvation, O God, protect me.

ISAIAH 50:6-7b   The Lord God Helps Me
I gave my back to those who struck me, and my cheeks to those who pulled out the beard; I did not hide my face from insult and spitting. The Lord GOD helps me; therefore I have not been disgraced.

PHILIPPIANS 4:12b, 13, 19   God Will Fully Satisfy Every Need
In any and all circumstances I have learned the secret . . . I can do all things through him who strengthens me . . . And my God will fully satisfy every need of yours according to his riches in glory in Christ Jesus.

MATTHEW 26:14-25   Today's Gospel Reading

> In his self-offering on the Cross, Jesus brings all the sin of the world deep within the love of God, and wipes it away. Accepting the Cross, entering into fellowship with Christ, means entering the realm of transformation.
> — JOSEPH RATZINGER, *JESUS OF NAZARETH*

EVENING REFLECTIONS

PSALM 74:18a, 20a, 21-22a—Remember this, O LORD, how the enemy scoffs . . . Have regard for your covenant . . . Do not let the downtrodden be put to shame; let the poor and needy praise your name. Rise up, O God, plead your cause.

PRAYER—My Lord and my God, you see my heart; and my desires are not hidden from you. I am encouraged and strengthened by your goodness to me today. I want to be yours and yours alone. O my God, my Savior, my Sanctifier, hear me, help me, and show mercy to me for Jesus Christ's sake. Amen. **JW**

THURSDAY
WEEK 6 † HOLY WEEK
LENTEN SEASON

PSALM 89:19-27 ▪ **ISAIAH 61:1-3, 6-9** ▪ **1 CORINTHIANS 11:27-32** ▪ **LUKE 4:16-21**

MORNING MEDITATIONS

PRAYER—Lord Jesus, abject, unknown, and despised, have mercy upon me, and let me not be ashamed to follow you. O Jesus, betrayed and sold at a vile price, have mercy on me and make me content to serve you as Master. O Jesus, blasphemed, accused, and wrongfully condemned, have mercy on me, and teach me to endure the contradiction of sinners. Amen. **JW**

PSALM 89:26-27—He shall cry to me, "You are my Father, my God, and the Rock of my salvation!" I will make him the firstborn, the highest of the kings of the earth.

ISAIAH 61:1-2a *The Lord Has Anointed Me*
The spirit of the Lord GOD is upon me, because the LORD has anointed me; he has sent me to bring good news to the oppressed, to bind up the brokenhearted, to proclaim liberty to the captives, and release to the prisoners; to proclaim the year of the LORD's favor.

1 CORINTHIANS 11:27-28a, 29 *Examine Yourselves*
Whoever, therefore, eats the bread or drinks the cup of the Lord in an unworthy manner will be answerable for the body and blood of the Lord. Examine yourselves . . . for all who eat and drink without discerning the body, eat and drink judgment against themselves.

LUKE 4:16-21 *Today's Gospel Reading*

> Christ is here! The Lord and Giver of life is here. The hour comes—and now is! "Today, if you hear his voice, do not harden your heart." Today, reach out hands of faith, and pray, "Jesus, think on me!" JAMES STEWART, *THE STRONG NAME*

EVENING REFLECTIONS

PSALM 142:5—I cry to you, O LORD; I say, "You are my refuge, my portion in the land of the living."

PRAYER—Give me, O Lord, a steadfast heart that no unworthy thought can diminish; give me an unconquered heart that no tribulation can sap; give me an upright heart that no base purpose can seduce. Bestow on me also, O Lord, understanding to know you, persistence to seek you, wisdom to find you and a faithfulness which may at the end embrace you. Amen. **St. Thomas Aquinas**

Good Friday

WEEK 6 † HOLY WEEK
LENTEN SEASON

PSALM 31:1-16 ▪ ISAIAH 52:13—53:12 ▪ 1 PETER 1:10-20 ▪ JOHN 19:16-37

MORNING MEDITATIONS

PRAYER—O Jesus, clothed with our reproach and shame, have mercy upon me, and let me not seek glory for myself. O Jesus, insulted, mocked, scourged, and bathed in blood, have mercy upon me, and let me run with patience the race set before me. Amen. *JW*

PSALM 31:11-12, 13b—I am the scorn of all my adversaries, a horror to my neighbors, an object of dread to my acquaintances; those who see me in the street flee from me. I have passed out of mind like one who is dead; I have become like a broken vessel . . . as they plot to take my life.

ISAIAH 53:3ab, 4a, 6b *Surely He Has Borne Our Infirmities*
He was despised and rejected by others; a man of suffering and acquainted with infirmity; and as one from whom others hide their faces . . . Surely he has borne our infirmities and carried our diseases . . . and the Lord has laid on him the iniquity of us all.

1 PETER 1:18-19 *The Precious Blood*
You know that you were ransomed from the futile ways inherited from your ancestors, not with perishable things like silver or gold, but with the precious blood of Christ, like that of a lamb without defect or blemish.

JOHN 19:16-37 *Today's Gospel Reading*

> In the Cross of Jesus, what the animal sacrifices had sought in vain to achieve actually occurred: atonement was made for the world. The "Lamb of God" took upon himself the sins of the world and wiped them away. God's relationship to the world, formerly distorted by sin, was now renewed. Reconciliation had been accomplished.
>
> JOSEPH RATZINGER, *JESUS OF NAZARETH*

EVENING REFLECTIONS

PSALM 40:1, 13, 17b—I waited patiently for the Lord; he inclined to me and heard my cry . . . Be pleased, O Lord, to deliver me; O Lord, make haste to help me . . . You are my help and my deliverer; do not delay, O my God.

READ: JOHN 19:38-42

Holy Saturday

WEEK 6 † HOLY WEEK
LENTEN SEASON

PSALM 16:5-11 ▪ GENESIS 22:1-18 ▪ HEBREWS 4:1-16 ▪ NO GOSPEL READING

MORNING MEDITATIONS

PRAYER—O Jesus, crowned with thorns, burdened with my sin, overwhelmed with injuries, hanging on the accursed tree, bowing the head, surrendering your life to death, have mercy on me and conform me to your holy, humble, suffering spirit. Amen. *JW*

PSALM 16:9-11—Therefore my heart is glad, and my soul rejoices; my body also rests secure. For you do not give me up to Sheol, or let your faithful one see the Pit. You show me the path of life. In your presence there is fullness of joy; in your right hand are pleasures forevermore.

GENESIS 22:7-8   *God Will Provide the Lamb*
Isaac said to his father Abraham, "Father!" And he said, "Here I am, my son." He said, "The fire and the wood are here, but where is the lamb for a burnt offering?" Abraham said, "God himself will provide the lamb for a burnt offering, my son." So the two of them walked on together.

HEBREWS 4:15-16   *Mercy and Grace in Time of Need*
For we do not have a high priest who is unable to sympathize with our weaknesses, but we have one who in every respect has been tested as we are, yet without sin. Let us therefore approach the throne of grace with boldness, so that we may receive mercy and find grace to help in time of need.

THERE IS NO READING OF THE GOSPEL TODAY.

> Christ chose the road of the cross deliberately, with one end in view. His death, he knew, would flash into the sinner's self-created darkness a light that would never be put out; and we would understand at last what sin is in its essential nature, and what it means to God . . . absolute sinless purity went down into the uncovered hell of a whole world's iniquity, and God was forsaken by God.   JAMES STEWART, *THE STRONG NAME*

EVENING REFLECTIONS

PSALM 27:13-14—I believe that I shall see the goodness of the LORD in the land of the living. Wait for the LORD; be strong, and let your heart take courage; wait for the LORD!

READ: ROMANS 8:1-11

WEEK ONE
Easter Season

Ashes to Fire Week 7

Sunday: Where Is He?

Read the gospel passages from John 20:1-18 and the devotional reflection titled "Where Is He?" then respond to the discussion prompts in the Reflective Journaling section.

THE MUSIC OF ASHES TO FIRE

Week 7: "Hope Is In the Grave" (Track 8)

Monday through Saturday

IN THE MORNING:

A personal daily devotional guide includes prayer, a reading from the Old Testament, the Psalms, the Epistles, and the Gospels for each day of the week.

In addition to the daily psalm, this week's readings come from Isaiah, Acts, and the gospels of Mark, Luke, and John.

Inspirational quotes from men and women of faith keep us in contact with our shared Christian heritage.

IN THE EVENING:

An evening psalm and prayer become preludes to nighttime rest and renewal.

RESURRECTION SUNDAY

Easter Season—Week One
Where Is He?

A devotional reflection based on John 20:1-18

*R*ead the gospel passage first, then the devotional reflection that follows. The discussion prompts at the end will help prepare you for Sunday school and small-group sessions.

It has the elements of a good mystery story—a missing body, investigators poring over evidence, an eerie encounter, and a surprise resolution. A woman walked alone from her home in town to the outskirts in the dark predawn hours. Sleep and rest had eluded her that night as her mind raced across the tragic events of the last few days. With only moonlight to guide her (for she did not want to attract attention by using a torch or lamp), she fled from shadow to shadow to the place she had been told his body had been laid.

"What will it be like?" she thought. "Will the guards be patrolling?" She stood aside in the shadows to look toward the cave-become-tomb. The moonlight shone on the big boulder. But something was odd. "The stone is dislodged! Oh, no! They have moved him to some undisclosed place!" She turned hastily to go and tell Peter and John about this distressing news. "Perhaps they have the authority to do something about it," she thought.

On hearing Mary's startling news, Peter and John left running, Peter struggling to keep up with the youthful John. John got to the tomb first and peeked inside but saw only linens lying about. Then he waited at the entrance for his senior companion to arrive at the scene. Peter assumed control and went into the tomb. Indeed, no one was there. Peter observed the burial strips and head cloth, noting that they were neatly arranged or folded. "This indicates that there was no violence or hurried departure," he thought. "And why did they not remove the body in the graveclothes?" This was a puzzle to Peter.

Quietly John entered the tomb and viewed the evidence. Something—intuition? revelation? convergence of clues?—clicked in his mind. Jesus had always said such strange things, he remembered, and now it was beginning to make sense! What Jesus had said had really come true! Perhaps as Peter and John returned after their investigation, John tried to explain to Peter what he figured out had happened in that tomb.

During Peter and John's investigation, Mary remained outside the tomb, crying over the loss and removal, she thought, of Jesus' body. When Peter and John decided to leave, Mary stayed and dared to go to look into the tomb herself. Through her tears she was startled to see two figures dressed in white sitting on the slab where Jesus' body had lain. She may have blinked, hoping the "vision" would disappear. But then they spoke to her, "Why are you crying?"

She told them what she knew of the scene. "They have taken away my Lord," she said, "and I do not know where they have laid him" (John 20:13). Then, sensing another's presence, she turned around and saw Jesus himself standing there, but she did not recognize him. This person asked her the same question, "Why are you [crying]? Whom are you looking for?" (v. 15). Still befuddled, Mary pled with the person whom she thought was the gardener, "If you have carried him away, tell me where you have laid him, and I will take him away" (v. 15). She had no clue to this mystery until she heard him speak, "Mary!" (v. 16a).

"Rabbouni!" (v. 16b). Bells rang. Memories exploded in her mind. As she rushed to embrace him, Jesus cautioned her, "Do not touch me" (i.e., "Don't disturb the evidence"; see v. 17). He told her to go and tell his disciples. She could hardly contain her news: "I have seen the Lord" (v. 18).

Every good mystery story has a satisfying resolution. At the end, justice is served and wrongs are righted in fiction. But in the reality of our lives, what we thought was secure becomes dislodged. We are taken by circumstances that disrupt the flow of the expected and routine:

- The pink slip at work—what will we do? What about the mortgage? Will we lose the house?
- Our financial insecurity looms large. Where is Jesus?
- The diagnosis at the doctor's office—is there a cure? How long does she have? Can we afford the medication? Our threatened health distresses us. Where is Jesus?

- The broken vows—is hope gone? Where will I go? How will I manage? Our broken relationships devastate us. Where is Jesus?
- The wayward child—where did I go wrong? Who is she with? Will he be arrested? Our family harmony has gone awry. Where is Jesus?
- The telephone call in the night—the wrenching separation of death. Can this be true? Take me to him. I have to get there. Earthly love is shattered with finality. Where is Jesus?

Like Mary at the tomb that Easter Sunday, our sorrows, fears, and pain blur our vision. We do not recognize Jesus standing there with us. But he still knows our names: "Mary," "Julio," "Sun Ye," "Abdul" (see 10:3). On this day may we listen for our name and recognize him and then be ready to go and tell, "I have seen the Lord."

—Helen Metcalfe

After reading the passage from John 20:1-18 and the devotional reflection "Where Is He?" you may also want to read the following related passages:

Isaiah 65:17-25; Psalm 118:1-2, 14-24;
1 Corinthians 15:19-26

The discussion prompts that follow will help prepare you to participate in your Sunday school class or small-group study. Use your Reflective Journaling section to record any other insights that come to you as you read the gospel lesson and the devotional reflection.

DISCUSSION PROMPT NO. 1: JOHN 20:1-18

Mary, and later Peter and John, all arrive at Jesus' tomb to find it empty. Each one has a different reaction. In what ways are their reactions similar to those who confront the reality of Christ's resurrection today?

DISCUSSION PROMPT NO. 2: JOHN 20:1-18

Both the angels and Jesus ask Mary the same question, "Woman, why are you weeping?" (v. 15). Have you ever felt God's compassionate presence in the midst of your grief and fear? What did you learn?

DISCUSSION PROMPT NO. 3: JOHN 20:1-18

Why do you think Mary only recognized Jesus when he spoke her name?

DISCUSSION PROMPT NO. 4: JOHN 20:1-18

Mary's simple witness, "I have seen the Lord!" (v. 18), is a profound testimony to a divine encounter. Have you heard or seen the power of a personal witness? Have you testified of your faith in Christ? When? How was it received?

DISCUSSION PROMPT NO. 5: DEVOTIONAL REFLECTION

Have you had an experience where your security was shaken and unexpected circumstances disrupted the flow of your life? Did you discover that God was nearer than you thought? How did God reveal his presence to you?

Reflective Journaling

MONDAY — WEEK 1 EASTER SEASON

PSALM 93 ▪ ISAIAH 43:1-7 ▪ ACTS 2:14, 22-28 ▪ LUKE 24:1-7

MORNING MEDITATIONS

PRAYER—O God, by my love for you may my soul be fixed against its tendency to be inconstant. May this holy flame always warm my heart, that I may serve you with all my might, and consume all selfish desires that I may possess a holy regard for you alone. Amen. **JW**

PSALM 93:1a, 4-5—The Lord is king, he is robed in majesty . . . More majestic than the thunders of mighty waters, more majestic than the waves of the sea, majestic on high is the Lord! Your decrees are very sure; holiness befits your house, O Lord, forevermore.

ISAIAH 43:2-3a *I Am Your Savior*
When you pass through the waters, I will be with you . . . when you walk through fire you shall not be burned, and the flame shall not consume you. For I am the Lord your God, the Holy One of Israel, your Savior.

ACTS 2:23-24 *God Raised Him Up*
This man, handed over to you according to the definite plan and foreknowledge of God, you crucified and killed by the hands of those outside the law. But God raised him up, having freed him from death, because it was impossible for him to be held in its power.

LUKE 24:1-7 *Today's Gospel Reading*

> He rose from the dead and cried out . . . "I am the Christ. It is I who destroyed death, who triumphed over the enemy, who trampled Hades underfoot, who bound the strong one and snatched man away to the heights of heaven. I am the Christ."
>
> ST. MELITO OF SARDIS, *HOMILY 100-102*

EVENING REFLECTIONS

PSALM 16:1, 9-11—Protect me, O God, for in you I take refuge. . . . My heart is glad, and my soul rejoices . . . For you do not give me up to Sheol, or let your faithful one see the Pit. You show me the path of life. In your presence there is fullness of joy; in your right hand are pleasures forevermore.

PRAYER—Lord, now that we have come to the setting of the sun and see the evening light, we give praise to God: Father, Son and Holy Spirit. Worthy are you at all times to be worshipped with holy voices, O Risen Christ and giver of life; therefore the world glorifies you. Amen. **JW**

TUESDAY — WEEK 1, EASTER SEASON

PSALM 33:4-5, 18-22 ▪ **ISAIAH 43:8-13** ▪ **ACTS 2:29-41** ▪ **LUKE 24:8-12**

MORNING MEDITATIONS

PRAYER—O God, I bless you that even after many refusals of your grace, you still had patience with me. You have preserved me through the night, and given me yet another day to live in repentant faith. Accept my thanks and praise. Amen. *JW*

PSALM 33:4-5a, 21-22—The word of the Lord is upright, and all his work is done in faithfulness. He loves righteousness and justice . . . Our heart is glad in him, because we trust in his holy name. Let your steadfast love, O Lord, be upon us, even as we hope in you.

ISAIAH 43:11-12a, 13ab *Besides Me There Is No Savior*
I, I am the Lord, and besides me there is no savior. I declared and saved and proclaimed . . . I am God, and also henceforth I am He; there is no one who can deliver from my hand.

ACTS 2:36 *Both Lord and Messiah*
Therefore let the entire house of Israel know with certainty that God has made him both Lord and Messiah, this Jesus whom you crucified.

LUKE 24:8-12 *Today's Gospel Reading*

> The Egyptians . . . who stand for darkness and suffering, are an apt symbol for the sins that harass us . . . The liberation of the children of Israel, and the journey by which they were led to the promised homeland, correspond to the mystery of our redemption, through which we make our way to the brightness of our heavenly home.
>
> ST. BEDE, *COMMENTARY ON 1 PETER*

EVENING REFLECTIONS

PSALM 111:1a, 9-10—Praise the Lord! . . . He sent redemption to his people; he has commanded his covenant forever. Holy and awesome is his name. The fear of the Lord is the beginning of wisdom; all those who practice it have a good understanding. His praise endures forever.

PRAYER—My Father, my God, I am in your hand; and may I rejoice above all things in simply being there. Do with me what seems good to you; just let me love you with all my heart, mind, soul, and strength. Amen. *JW*

WEDNESDAY
WEEK 1 EASTER SEASON

PSALM 105:1-6, 43-45 ▪ ISAIAH 43:14-21 ▪ ACTS 3:1-10 ▪ LUKE 24:13-35

MORNING MEDITATIONS

PRAYER—Almighty God, I bless you from my heart. O Savior of the World, God of God, Light of Light, you have destroyed the power of the devil, you have overcome death, and you sit at the right hand of the Father. Be today my light and peace and make me a new creature, through Christ my Lord. Amen. *JW*

PSALM 105:1-3—O give thanks to the Lord, call on his name, make known his deeds among the peoples. Sing to him, sing praises to him; tell of all his wonderful works. Glory in his holy name; let the hearts of those who seek the Lord rejoice.

ISAIAH 43:14a, 18-19 *A New Thing*
Thus says the Lord, your Redeemer, the Holy One of Israel . . . Do not remember the former things, or consider the things of old. I am about to do a new thing; now it springs forth, do you not perceive it? I will make a way in the wilderness and rivers in the desert.

ACTS 3:3, 6, 9a, 10b *Stand Up and Walk*
When [the lame man] saw Peter and John about to go into the temple, he asked them for alms . . . But Peter said, "I have no silver or gold, but what I have I give you; in the name of Jesus Christ of Nazareth, stand up and walk" . . . All the people . . . were filled with wonder and amazement.

LUKE 24:13-35 *Today's Gospel Reading*

> "By my flesh I have redeemed the flesh of all men. For in my death, death will die, and fallen human nature will rise again with me." There was never any other way to destroy the one who had the power of death, and therefore death itself. Christ had to give himself up for us all.   ST. CYRIL OF ALEXANDER, *COMMENTARY ON S. JOHN'S GOSPEL*

EVENING REFLECTIONS

PSALM 115:1, 12a, 13—Not to us, O Lord, not to us, but to your name give glory, for the sake of your steadfast love and your faithfulness . . . The Lord has been mindful of us . . . he will bless those who fear the Lord, both great and small.

PRAYER—O Lord, visit this place I pray, and drive far from it all the snares of the enemy; may your holy angels dwell with me and guard me in peace, and may your blessings rest upon all of us always; through Jesus Christ, our Lord. Amen. *JW*

THURSDAY
WEEK I · EASTER SEASON

PSALM 147 ▪ ISAIAH 44:1-8 ▪ ACTS 3:11-26 ▪ LUKE 24:35-48

MORNING MEDITATIONS

PRAYER—Eternal God, my Sovereign Lord, I acknowledge all I am, all I have is yours. I humbly thank you for all the blessings you have bestowed upon me—for creating me in your own image, for redeeming me by the death of your blessed Son, and for the assistance of the Holy Spirit. Amen. **JW**

PSALM 147:1ab, 15, 19—Praise the Lord! How good it is to sing praises to our God . . . He sends out his command to the earth; his word runs swiftly. . . He declares his word to Jacob, his statutes and ordinances to Israel.

ISAIAH 44:6, 8 *I Am the First and I Am the Last*
Thus says the Lord, the King of Israel, and his Redeemer, the Lord of hosts: I am the first and I am the last; besides me there is no god . . . Do not fear, or be afraid . . . You are my witnesses! Is there any god besides me? There is no other rock; I know not one.

ACTS 3:19-20 *Turn to God*
Repent, therefore, and turn to God so that your sins may be wiped out, so that times of refreshing may come from the presence of the Lord, and that he may send the Messiah appointed for you, that is, Jesus.

LUKE 24:35-48 *Today's Gospel Reading*

> Revelation is not a collection of statements—revelation is Christ himself. He is the Logos, the all-embracing Word in which God declares himself and whom we therefore call the Son of God . . . the *Word* is always greater than the *words* and is never exhausted by the words.
>
> JOSEPH RATZINGER, *ON THE WAY TO JESUS CHRIST*

EVENING REFLECTIONS

PSALM 148:1, 11, 13—Praise the Lord! Praise the Lord from the heavens; praise him in the heights! . . . Kings of the earth and all peoples, princes and all rulers of the earth! . . . Let them praise the name of the Lord, for his name alone is exalted.

PRAYER—O God, as darkness falls you renew your promise to reveal the light of your presence. May your Word be a lantern to my feet and a light unto my path that I may walk as a child of light and sing your praise throughout the world, in Jesus' name. Amen. **JW**

FRIDAY
WEEK 1 EASTER SEASON

PSALM 118:1-2, 4, 22-27a ▪ ISAIAH 44:21-28 ▪ ACTS 4:1-12 ▪ JOHN 21:1-14

MORNING MEDITATIONS

PRAYER—Keep us, O Lord, as long as we remain on this earth, in a serious seeking after you, and in an affectionate walking with you, every day of our lives so that when you come, we may be found waiting and longing for you, our Lord, our glorious God for ever. ***Richard Baxter***

PSALM 118:22-24—The stone that the builders rejected has become the chief cornerstone. This is the Lord's doing; it is marvelous in our eyes. This is the day that the Lord has made; let us rejoice and be glad in it.

ISAIAH 44:21-22 *I Have Swept Away Your Transgressions*
Remember these things, O Jacob, and Israel, for you are my servant; I formed you, you are my servant; O Israel, you will not be forgotten by me. I have swept away your transgressions like a cloud, and your sins like mist; return to me, for I have redeemed you.

ACTS 4:10-11 *By the Name of Jesus Christ*
Let it be known to all of you, and to all the people of Israel, that this man is standing before you in good health by the name of Jesus Christ of Nazareth, whom you crucified, whom God raised from the dead. This Jesus is "the stone that was rejected by you, the builders; it has become the cornerstone."

JOHN 21:1-14 *Today's Gospel Reading*

> When we come to know God the Father, as Jesus has portrayed him, then suddenly we perceive his radiant words in an entirely different light; then everything makes sense and becomes believable; then the Father leads us to the Son, just as the Son previously led us to the Father. —JOSEPH RATZINGER, *ON THE WAY TO JESUS CHRIST*

EVENING REFLECTIONS

PSALM 118:17, 19, 28b—I shall not die, but I shall live, and recount the deeds of the Lord . . . Open to me the gates of righteousness, that I may enter through them and give thanks to the Lord . . . You are my God, I will extol you.

PRAYER—Merciful God, whatever you may deny me, do not deny me of your love. Save me from the idolatry of loving the world, or any of the things of the world. Let me never love any creature, but for your sake and in subordination to your love. Take full possession of my heart, raise your throne in it, and rule there as you do in heaven. Amen. ***JW***

SATURDAY
WEEK I
EASTER SEASON

PSALM 118:1, 14-21 ▪ ISAIAH 45:8-25 ▪ ACTS 4:13-21 ▪ MARK 16:9-15

MORNING MEDITATIONS

PRAYER—O Lord, you did not please yourself even though all things were created for your pleasure. Let some portion of your Spirit descend on me, so that I may deny myself and follow you, in Jesus' name, Amen. *JW*

PSALM 118:14-15, 17—The LORD is my strength and my might; he has become my salvation. There are glad songs of victory in the tents of the righteous: The right hand of the Lord does valiantly . . . I shall not die, but I shall live, and recount the deeds of the LORD.

ISAIAH 45:21b-22, 23b *Every Knee Shall Bow*
There is no other god besides me, a righteous God and a Savior; there is no one besides me. Turn to me and be saved, all the ends of the earth! For I am God, and there is no other . . . To me every knee shall bow, every tongue shall swear.

ACTS 4:18-20 *We Cannot Keep from Speaking*
So they called them and ordered them not to speak or teach at all in the name of Jesus. But Peter and John answered them, "Whether it is right in God's sight to listen to you rather than God, you must judge; for we cannot keep from speaking about what we have seen and heard."

MARK 16:9-15 *Today's Gospel Reading*

> Only Christ can hold together and unify the whole; when we speak of Christ, we must, of course, always see the Trinitarian mystery in the background; he comes from the Father, and he works at present in all of history through the Holy Spirit, who bears witness to Christ and guides all believers in all the truth. JOSEPH RATZINGER, *ON THE WAY TO JESUS CHRIST*

EVENING REFLECTIONS

PSALM 104:1, 33a, 34—Bless the LORD, O my soul. O LORD my God, you are very great. You are clothed with honor and majesty . . . I will sing to the LORD as long as I live . . . May my meditation be pleasing to him, for I rejoice in the LORD.

PRAYER—High King of Heaven, though I live on earth, I desire your will to be done in my life as it is done in heaven. I will join my song with those of saints and angels in a hymn of unending praise: Holy, holy, holy is the Lord; heaven and earth are full of your glory. Glory to you, O Lord. Amen. *JW*

WEEK TWO
Easter Season

Ashes to Fire Week 8

Sunday: Life's Locked-Door Seasons

Read the gospel passage from John 20:19-31 and the devotional reflection titled "Life's Locked-Door Seasons," then respond to the discussion prompts in the Reflective Journaling section.

THE MUSIC OF ASHES TO FIRE

Week 8: "When Love Shows Up" (Track 9)

Monday through Saturday

IN THE MORNING:

A personal daily devotional guide includes prayer, a reading from the Old Testament, the Psalms, the Epistles, and the Gospels for each day of the week.

In addition to the daily psalm, this week's readings come from Isaiah, Acts, and the gospel of John.

Inspirational quotes from men and women of faith keep us in contact with our shared Christian heritage.

IN THE EVENING:

An evening psalm and prayer become preludes to nighttime rest and renewal.

SUNDAY

Easter Season—Week Two
Life's Locked-Door Seasons

A devotional reflection based on John 20:19-31

Read the gospel passage first, then the devotional reflection that follows. The discussion prompts at the end will help prepare you for Sunday school and small-group sessions.

Today's passage is usually read on what many call Low Sunday, which falls on the Sunday after Easter. The origins of this name are mixed. There is, for instance, some association with the idea that the Sunday following Easter, on which the eight-day Easter celebration ends, is lower in importance than Easter; the name also may be a simple acknowledgment that after all the celebration of Easter the return to the regular life of the church is a lower celebration. Whatever the origin, the choice to have John 20:19-31 read on this day seems appropriate both for the traditional rhythm of church life and the metaphorical applications to our own experiences of lowness.

In either case, there is a teasing out of this Easter faith in the midst of regular day-to-day life. The pastor who comes back to the flower-stripped church is still proclaiming the good news: "Christ is risen!" Yet the message can sometimes be delivered with a weary voice, and the exclamation point can at times seem more like a question mark. As an Easter people we move into different seasons of life when we experience that same weariness and questioning.

In the Scripture reading, the disciples were afraid and locked the doors (v. 19). In my journey there are seasons when that just seems to be the best choice. The good news of the resurrection can feel like a distant whisper, and the very real sense of danger can swirl about my mind and heart. The locked doors are an attempt to create protection, to chase away vulnerability, to be safe. The locked doors can also become a way of living. Nothing can get through and cause harm.

The beauty of the story is that the locked door is no obstacle to the risen Christ. Jesus came, stood among them, and said, "Peace be with you" (v. 21)—the very same words he had said at the Last Supper before all the chaos, death, and destruction had occurred (see 14:27). And now he utters them again, proclaiming a living word over every experience of chaos, death, and destruction we might know. And this living word is true because it comes forth from the One who has vanquished death itself. Jesus shows up when we have locked every door and have curled up in our beds determined not to rise again. When the decorations of life have been stripped away, the resurrected Christ comes and breathes new life and says, "Peace be with you."

"Peace be with you. As the Father has sent me, so I send you." When he had said this, he breathed on them and said to them, "Receive the Holy Spirit. If you forgive the sins of any, they are forgiven them; if you retain the sins of any, they are retained." (20:21-23)

What can these words mean to a people or person who has been hunkered down behind locked doors? What did this mean for these disciples? Perhaps the connection between peace and forgiveness challenges us about the half peace we often are content to receive. This peace the risen Christ offers is not just a settled notion that "I am safe" but something that goes deeper than a sigh of relief from whatever immediate sense of danger that has overwhelmed us. These words are offering peace and healing to the damage that can occur when we have been utterly afraid—the deep damage of harboring hate, bitterness, and anger against those people we feared would cause harm to us or those we love. This peace Jesus gives transforms our hearts and lives, allowing us again to love, move about our world, and live joyfully. We can all be tempted to stop enjoying life, to forget what it means to love, and to withhold forgiveness. But that does not seem to be an option when we're in the presence of the resurrected Lord. Rather, his peace, the breath of the Spirit, and the offer of forgiveness seem to all be part of our fully knowing the resurrection promise of new life.

Of course, it can be hard work—not on the part of our personal ability to claim God's peace and forgiveness. Rather, it is sometimes difficult to let Christ speak those words *over us*, breathe his life *into us*, and forgive again and again *through us*.

The beauty of this story in John 20 has not ended. Jesus continues to appear and bring resurrection life into the locked-door seasons of our lives. Thomas becomes a representative of many things: our doubts, our inability to experience the reality claimed by others, and our past experiences that keep us from fully knowing new life (vv. 24-29). And yet once again we have this image of Jesus showing up despite the closed doors and offering this profound, life-changing peace to our troubled hearts—peace beyond the immediate sense of danger, peace that reaches out to the one ignored, peace that embraces the one needing the reassurance that this resurrection life is not just a promise but something to be touched, known, and embraced.

The witness of the faithful is that the more they handle Scripture, the more God seems to handle them; the more they hold and receive Communion, the more they are held and received by God; the more they are open to being faithful followers of Christ, the more they receive the ministry of Christ through his wounds; and the more they pour themselves out in prayer, the more they know the very real presence of Christ offering new life and forgiveness. The faithfulness of Christ to show up in our locked-door seasons when we desperately cry, "I need to know the reality of your presence once again," comes, not because we demand it, but because the resurrected Christ desires to make his presence known again and again with the words, "Peace be with you."

Blessed Easter on this Low Sunday! —Mary Rearick Paul

After reading the passage from John 20:19-31 and the devotional reflection "Life's Locked-Door Seasons," you may also want to read the following related passages:

Acts 5:27-32; Psalm 118:1-2, 14-29; and Revelation 1:4-8

The discussion prompts that follow will help prepare you to participate in your Sunday school class or small-group study. Use your Reflective Journaling section to record any other insights that come to you as you read the gospel lesson and the devotional reflection.

DISCUSSION PROMPT NO. 1: JOHN 20:19-31

What transformation took place in the disciples when Jesus appeared? How does a sense of Christ's presence transform our lives?

DISCUSSION PROMPT NO. 2: JOHN 20:19-31

Each time Jesus appears he says to the disciples, "Peace be with you!" (vv. 19, 21, 26). Why do you think this was an important message for them to hear?

DISCUSSION PROMPT NO. 3: JOHN 20:19-31

Thomas demanded extraordinary proof and when it was given he made an extraordinary confession, "My Lord and my God!" (v. 28). Jesus, however, says that "blessed are those who have not seen and yet have come to believe" (v. 29). Do we need to see to believe? Or is it only when we believe that we can see?

DISCUSSION PROMPT NO. 4: JOHN 20:19-31

John said that he recorded the things that he did in his gospel "that you may come to believe that Jesus is the Messiah, the Son of God" (v. 31). How have you come to believe that God's Word is true?

DISCUSSION PROMPT NO. 5: DEVOTIONAL REFLECTION

What do you think the writer means when she says that the more you "handle Scripture, the more God seems to handle" you; the more you "hold and receive Communion, the more [you] are held and received by God"; the more you are "open to being [a] faithful [follower] of Christ" and "pour [yourself] out in prayer," the more you "know the very real presence of Christ"? Have you found it true in your life? Explain. In what ways does Christ reveal his presence in your life?

Reflective Journaling

MONDAY
WEEK 2 • EASTER SEASON

PSALM 2 • ISAIAH 46 • ACTS 4:23-31 • JOHN 3:1-8

MORNING MEDITATIONS

PRAYER—O God, Infinite Goodness, confirm your past mercies to me by enabling me for what remains of my life to be more faithful than I have been up until now to your great command to love as I have been loved. Let me not rest in any external devotion, nor trust in words or sighs or tears. Let me know and feel what it is to love you with all my heart. Amen. **JW**

PSALM 2:7-8—I will tell of the decree of the LORD: He said to me, "You are my son; today I have begotten you. Ask of me, and I will make the nations your heritage, and the ends of the earth your possession."

ISAIAH 46:12-13   *I Bring Near My Deliverance*
Listen to me you, stubborn of heart, you who are far from deliverance: I bring near my deliverance, it is not far off, and my salvation will not tarry; I will put salvation in Zion, for Israel my glory.

ACTS 4:29-30   *Stretch Out Your Hand to Heal*
And now, Lord, look at their threats, and grant to your servants to speak your word with all boldness, while you stretch out your hand to heal, and signs and wonders are performed through the name of your holy servant Jesus.

JOHN 3:1-8   *Today's Gospel Reading*

> Jesus could have lived his life in a small village. He could have had the comforts of home. He could have lived to a ripe old age. He could have settled for popularity. But a fire burned within him. A mission compelled him, and so he gave himself away. He "went about doing good" and saying to all who would hear and heed, "Come, follow me."
>
> JOHN BOWLING, GRACE-FULL LEADERSHIP

EVENING REFLECTIONS

PSALM 4:6b, 7a, 8—Let the light of your face shine on us, O LORD! . . . You have put gladness in my heart . . . I will both lie down and sleep in peace; for you alone, O LORD, make me lie down in safety.

PRAYER—Merciful God, whatever you may deny me, do not deny me of your love. Save me from the idolatry of loving the world, or any of the things of the world. Take full possession of my heart, raise your throne in it, and rule there as you do in heaven. Amen. **JW**

TUESDAY — WEEK 2 EASTER SEASON

PSALM 93:1-5 ▪ ISAIAH 48:1-17 ▪ ACTS 4:32-37 ▪ JOHN 3:7b-15

MORNING MEDITATIONS

PRAYER—Jesus, my Savior, let your love rule my heart without a rival. Let it dispose all my thoughts, words, and works; for then only can I fulfill my duty and your command of loving you with all my heart, and mind, and soul, and strength. Amen. *JW*

PSALM 93:1-2—The Lord is king, he is robed in majesty; the Lord . . . is girded with strength. He has established the world; it shall never be moved; your throne is established from of old; you are from everlasting.

ISAIAH 48:12-13b, 17   *I Lead You in the Way You Should Go*
Listen to me, O Jacob, and Israel, whom I called: I am He; I am the first, and I am the last. My hand laid the foundation of the earth, and my right hand spread out the heavens . . . Thus says the Lord, your Redeemer, the Holy One of Israel: I am the Lord your God . . . who leads you in the way you should go.

ACTS 4:32a, 33   *Great Grace Was upon Them All*
Now the whole group of those who believed were of one heart and soul . . . With great power the apostles gave their testimony to the resurrection of the Lord Jesus, and great grace was upon them all.

JOHN 3:7b-15   *Today's Gospel Reading*

> Just as a beautiful house built upon a poor foundation cannot provide a stable and secure habitation, neither can a veneer of personality cover or compensate for weak character. "In the end, your integrity is all you've got." Solomon said it wisely . . . : "Above all else, guard your heart, for it is the wellspring of life."   —JOHN BOWLING, *GRACE-FULL LEADERSHIP*

EVENING REFLECTIONS

PSALM 11:4, 7—The Lord is in his holy temple; the Lord's throne is in heaven. His eyes behold, his gaze examines humankind . . . The Lord is righteous; he loves righteous deeds; the upright shall behold his face.

PRAYER—O my Father, my God, I ask you to deliver me from any passions that obstruct my knowledge and love of you. Let none of them find a way into my heart, but instead, give me a meek and gentle spirit. Reign in my heart; may I always be your servant and love you with all my heart. Amen. *JW*

WEDNESDAY
WEEK 2 — EASTER SEASON

PSALM 34:1-10 ▪ ISAIAH 49:1-7 ▪ ACTS 5:17-26 ▪ JOHN 3:16-21

MORNING MEDITATIONS

PRAYER—Lord God, may I always honor your glorious name, and love the creation you have made. May your infinite goodness and greatness be adored by angels and humankind alike. May all who call themselves by your name catch a glimpse of that goodness. Amen. **JW**

PSALM 34:1-3—I will bless the Lord at all times; his praise shall continually be in my mouth. My soul makes its boast in the Lord; let the humble hear and be glad. O magnify the Lord with me, and let us exalt his name together.

ISAIAH 49:5a, 6   *I Give You as a Light to the Nations*
And now the Lord says, who formed me in the womb to be his servant, . . . "It is too light a thing that you should be my servant to raise up the tribes of Jacob only and to restore the survivors of Israel; I will give you as a light to the nations, that my salvation may reach to the end of the earth."

ACTS 5:19-21   *Tell the People the Whole Message*
During the night an angel of the Lord opened the prison doors, brought them out, and said, "Go, stand in the temple and tell the people the whole message about this life." When they heard this, they entered the temple at daybreak and went on with their teaching.

JOHN 3:16-21   *Today's Gospel Reading*

> "Guard your heart." Put a sentinel on duty. Watch it carefully. Protect it. Pay attention to it. Keep it clean. Clear away the debris. This is a command. And there is an intense priority here—"above all else." To remember God and our ultimate accountability to him is life's highest priority.
>
> JOHN BOWLING, *GRACE-FULL LEADERSHIP*

EVENING REFLECTIONS

PSALM 13:3, 5—Consider and answer me, O Lord my God! Give light to my eyes, or I will sleep the sleep of death . . . I trusted in your steadfast love; my heart shall rejoice in your salvation.

PRAYER—O God, deliver me from an idolatrous self-love. I know that this sin is the root of all evil. I praise you that in your infinite mercy you have granted me the grace to overcome it. I know you have made me, not to do my own will, but yours. Amen. **JW**

THURSDAY
WEEK 2
EASTER SEASON

PSALM 34:11-22 ▪ ISAIAH 51:1-8 ▪ ACTS 5:27-33 ▪ JOHN 3:31-36

MORNING MEDITATIONS

PRAYER—Eternal God, you have commanded me to renounce self. So give me strength, and I will obey your will. My choice, my desire is to love myself and others in and for you alone. May your mighty arm establish me, strengthen me, and settle me as both the foundation and pillar of my love. Amen. *JW*

PSALM 34:15, 22—The eyes of the Lord are on the righteous, and his ears are open to their cry . . . The Lord redeems the life of his servants; none of those who take refuge in him will be condemned.

ISAIAH 51:3   *Joy and Gladness Will Be Found in Zion*
For the Lord will comfort Zion; he will comfort all her waste places, and will make her wilderness like Eden, her desert like the garden of the Lord; joy and gladness will be found in her, thanksgiving and the voice of song.

ACTS 5:29-31   *The God of Our Ancestors Raised Up Jesus*
Peter and the apostles answered, "We must obey God rather than any human authority. The God of our ancestors raised up Jesus, whom you had killed by hanging him on a tree. God exalted him at his right hand as Leader and Savior that he might give repentance to Israel and forgiveness of sins."

JOHN 3:31-36   *Today's Gospel Reading*

> If we forget God, if we forget the One to whom we belong, if our hearts get cluttered and crowded and cramped, if we lose our way spiritually, then no other amount of remembering will make much difference . . . and so "above all else, guard your heart."
>
> JOHN BOWLING, *GRACE-FULL LEADERSHIP*

EVENING REFLECTIONS

PSALM 12:6-7—The promises of the Lord are promises that are pure, silver refined in a furnace . . . purified seven times. You, O Lord, will protect us; you will guard us from this generation forever.

PRAYER—O Lamb of God, be a guard to my desires so that I attach myself to nothing that will hinder an undivided love of you. O God, you have required of me that I love you with all my heart. Be both the assurance and the security of my heart's intention to be open to nothing except a complete love for you. Amen. *JW*

FRIDAY
WEEK 2 EASTER SEASON

PSALM 27:1-4, 11-14 ▪ ISAIAH 52:1-12 ▪ ACTS 5:34-42 ▪ JOHN 6:1-15

MORNING MEDITATIONS

PRAYER—O God, your lovingkindness reaches everything you have made, but especially to us who are made in your image with a capability of knowing and loving you eternally. May I not exclude anybody from my love today since they are the objects of your divine mercy, through Christ my Lord, Amen. *JW*

PSALM 27:11a, 13-14—Teach me your way, O Lord, and lead me on a level path . . . I believe that I shall see the goodness of the Lord in the land of the living. Wait for the Lord; be strong, and let your heart take courage; wait for the Lord!

ISAIAH 52:6-7 *My People Shall Know My Name*
Therefore my people shall know my name; therefore in that day they shall know that it is I who speak; here am I. How beautiful upon the mountains are the feet of the messenger who announces peace, who brings good news, who announces salvation, who says to Zion, "Your God reigns."

ACTS 5:34a, 35a, 38b-39a *If This Is of Human Origin, It Will Fail*
A Pharisee in the council named Gamaliel, a teacher of the law, respected by all the people . . . said to them, . . . "If this plan or this undertaking is of human origin, it will fail; but if it is of God, you will not be able to overthrow them."

JOHN 6:1-15 *Today's Gospel Reading*

> "Guard your heart, for it is the wellspring of life." Every person has an inner being, a center from which all of life flows . . . When the heart is pure, all that flows from it will be pure; but if the heart becomes bitter or sour or soiled, that which flows forth will also be bitter and sour and soiled. Life is lived inside out. JOHN BOWLING, *GRACE-FULL LEADERSHIP*

EVENING REFLECTIONS

PSALM 134:1-2—Come, bless the Lord, all you servants of the Lord, who stand by night in the house of the Lord! Lift up your hands in the holy place, and bless the Lord.

PRAYER—Father, let your love to me be the pattern of my love to my neighbor. You spared no expense to rescue me from the misery of my sinful past, so let me offer the benefit of the doubt to all those I know and love. May they, too, become your faithful servants, and may all Christians everywhere live up to the religion they profess. Amen. *JW*

SATURDAY
WEEK 2 EASTER SEASON

PSALM 33:1-5, 18-19 ▪ **ISAIAH 54:4-17** ▪ **ACTS 6:1-7** ▪ **JOHN 6:16-21**

MORNING MEDITATIONS

PRAYER—Lord of life, you have destroyed death through the resurrection of your Son Jesus Christ. I pray today that I may live in his presence and rejoice in the hope of eternal glory. Amen.

PSALM 33:1, 3a, 4, 5b—Rejoice in the Lord, O you righteous. Praise befits the upright . . . Sing to him a new song . . . For the word of the Lord is upright, and all his work is done in faithfulness . . . The earth is full of the steadfast love of the Lord.

ISAIAH 54:4ab, 17   Do Not Be Discouraged
Do not fear, for you will not be ashamed; do not be discouraged, for you will not suffer disgrace . . . No weapon that is fashioned against you shall prosper, and you shall confute every tongue that rises against you in judgment. This is the heritage of the servants of the Lord.

ACTS 6:3, 5   A Man Full of Faith and the Holy Spirit
Select from among yourselves seven men of good standing, full of the Spirit and of wisdom, whom we may appoint to this task . . . What they said pleased the whole community, and they chose Stephen, a man full of faith and the Holy Spirit, together with [others].

JOHN 6:16-21   Today's Gospel Reading

> Life is lived inside out. The world reverses that formula. People might think that if we have the right things on the outside—the right clothes, friends, possessions, and positions—then the inside will be happy and at peace. But that is not true, for the wellspring of life is from within, not without.
> — JOHN BOWLING, *GRACE-FULL LEADERSHIP*

EVENING REFLECTIONS

PSALM 117—Praise the Lord, all you nations! Extol him, all you peoples! For great is his steadfast love toward us, and the faithfulness of the Lord endures forever. Praise the Lord!

PRAYER—O God, forgive my enemies, and in due time make them my friends. Have mercy on all those who are afflicted in any way. Keep them patient in their sufferings. May we together take part in the joy of resurrection power through him who lives and reigns with you and the Holy Spirit, one God, world without end. Amen. **JW**

WEEK THREE
Easter Season

Ashes to Fire Week 9

Sunday: Hook or Crook?

Read the gospel passage from John 21:1-19 and the devotional reflection titled "Hook or Crook?" then respond to the discussion prompts in the Reflective Journaling section.

THE MUSIC OF ASHES TO FIRE

Week 9: "He Leadeth Me" (Track 10)

Monday through Saturday

IN THE MORNING:

A personal daily devotional guide includes prayer, a reading from the Old Testament, the Psalms, the Epistles, and the Gospels for each day of the week.

In addition to the daily psalm, this week's readings come from Isaiah, Acts, and the gospel of John.

Inspirational quotes from men and women of faith keep us in contact with our shared Christian heritage.

IN THE EVENING:

An evening psalm and prayer become preludes to nighttime rest and renewal.

SUNDAY

Easter Season—Week Three
Hook or Crook?

A devotional reflection based on John 21:1-19

*R*ead the gospel passage first, then the devotional reflection that follows. The discussion prompts at the end will help prepare you for Sunday school and small-group sessions.

English can be a difficult language to learn. For the past six years our church has provided free English as a second language classes to our neighbors, two-thirds of whom speak a language other than English as their first language. In English there are many figures of speech that often confuse and confound both English and non-English speakers.

One student who was frustrated with understanding figures of speech asked, "How can a *slim* chance and a *fat* chance be the same? How come a wise *man* and a wise *guy* are opposites? Why is it that when a house burns *up*, it burns *down*? How is it that you fill *in* a form by filling it *out* and that an alarm clock goes *off* by going *on*. And why, when I wind up my watch, I *start* it, but when I wind up this essay, I *end* it?"

There is an old figure of speech in English that says, "By hook or by crook." Have you ever heard that phrase? "By hook or by crook." It means "by whatever means possible" or "whatever it takes to get the job done."

It is sometimes suggested that this phrase derives from a custom in medieval England of allowing peasants to take any deadwood from the royal forest that they could reach with a shepherd's crook or a reaper's billhook. Others suggest that this phrase came into usage with the translation of the New Testament into English in 1380 by John Wycliffe. It is said that this phrase was derived from our scripture for today, John 21, which uses these two common items—the *hook* (the fishhook) and the *crook* (the shepherd's staff)—to symbolize two important ministries of the church: evangelism and nurture.

When Pope Benedict the Sixteenth was inaugurated at St. Peter's Square on April 24, 2005, he was given two items of clothing that represented these two ministries. First, he was given the fisherman's ring—which shows Peter fishing from a boat, symbolizing the call to be a *fisher of people*. Second, he was given a woolen cloak, placed on the shoulders, symbolizing the call to be *shepherd* of God's flock, the church.

John brings both of these images together in verses 1-19. And through Jesus' interaction with Peter in our scripture, John reveals something about the essential character of the mission of the Christian church: the Christian church is called to *shepherd* the flock of God and to be *fishers* of people, catching people with the good news of Jesus Christ.

Now these two tasks are not always easy to keep together. I'll be the first to admit that I'm no fisherman. I've thrown out a line a few times, with mixed results, but I don't know a whole lot about fishing.

And I'm no shepherd; I've never tended sheep. When I was in Ireland a few years back, I watched some shepherds in action, from a distance—a safe distance. Some of those sheep looked mighty mean. I've watched from a distance, but I've never literally shepherded sheep.

No, I'm no fisherman and I'm no shepherd, but it seems to me, as an outside observer, that these two tasks are somewhat mutually exclusive of each other. You're not going to be a very good fisherman if you spend all your time with your feet on the ground in the pasture with the sheep. And you're not going to be a very good shepherd if you are away from your flock, out at sea, far from shore, away from the pasture.

From my perspective it seems odd to put these two professions together. A *good* fisherman will be a *lousy* shepherd, and a *good* shepherd will be a *lousy* fisherman! It seems that a person would have to choose between these two professions, by hook *or* by crook.

Which will it be? There is a bit of a tension here, isn't there? This tension often exists between members of a church. There are those who believe the mission of the church is to be *fishers of people*—that evangelism is the number one priority for the church, reaching lost people with the good news of Jesus Christ. There are others who believe the mission of the church is to be *shepherds*—caring for and tending those who are already in the fold, nurturing, discipling, and loving the sheep. Sometimes we get downright disagreeable over which should take priority, the *fisherman's hook* or the *shepherd's crook*.

The reality is that we don't get to choose. The mission of the Christian church, represented in Jesus' commissioning of Peter, includes both. We are called to be *fishermen* and *shepherds*. And as we consider the mission of our church in these days, we must ensure that *both* aspects of the mission are included. Which means that *all* of us have to be involved in this work. Those who are gifted and passionate about *fishing*, and those who are gifted and passionate about *shepherding*. The mission of God can't be done by just one person or by just one ministry of the church. We need the whole people of God to complete the whole mission of God. By hook and by crook. —Grant Zweigle

After reading the passage from John 21:1-19 and the devotional reflection "Hook or Crook?" you may also want to read the following related passages:
Acts 9:1-20; Psalm 30; and Revelation 5:11-14

The discussion prompts that follow will help prepare you to participate in your Sunday school class or small-group study. Use your Reflective Journaling section to record any other insights that come to you as you read the gospel lesson and the devotional reflection.

DISCUSSION PROMPT NO. 1: JOHN 21:1-19
What do you think it was about the incident of the miraculous catch of fish that caused John to exclaim, "It is the Lord" (v. 7)?

DISCUSSION PROMPT NO. 2: JOHN 21:1-19
Why do you think Jesus prepared breakfast for the disciples? What might it have taught them about their future life and ministry?

DISCUSSION PROMPT NO. 3: JOHN 21:1-19
Why do you think Jesus asked Simon Peter three times, "Do you love me?" (v. 17). Was Jesus chastising Peter for his betrayal? Or, was Jesus testing the depth of his commitment? Have you ever felt challenged to "count the cost" of following Jesus?

DISCUSSION PROMPT NO. 4: JOHN 21:1-19
Jesus' command to Peter, "Follow me" (v. 19), is the same he extended to his disciples at the beginning (John 1:43). What do you believe it means to follow Jesus today?

DISCUSSION PROMPT NO. 5: DEVOTIONAL REFLECTION

The church's mission encompasses both those who are outside the church (evangelism) and those on the inside (discipleship). Have you discovered your place in the church's mission? What is it? How did you recognize God's field of service for you? If you don't yet have a specific field of service, are you seeking God's direction? How? Have you shared with other believers your desire to serve Christ in whatever way he may direct?

Reflective Journaling

MONDAY
WEEK 3 · EASTER SEASON

PSALM 119:25-32 ▪ ISAIAH 55 ▪ ACTS 6:8-15 ▪ JOHN 6:22-29

MORNING MEDITATIONS

PRAYER—Our Father in heaven, we are sure that there is nothing in us that could attract the love of One as holy and as just as you are. Yet you have declared your unchanging love for us in Jesus Christ. We thank you that nothing in the universe can prevent you from loving us. Amen.

PSALM 119:30-32—I have chosen the way of faithfulness; I set your ordinances before me. I cling to your decrees, O Lord; let me not be put to shame. I run the way of your commandments, for you enlarge my understanding.

ISAIAH 55:6-7   *Seek the Lord*
Seek the Lord while he may be found, call upon him while he is near; let the wicked forsake their way, and the unrighteous their thoughts; let them return to the Lord, that he may have mercy on them, and to our God, for he will abundantly pardon.

ACTS 6:8, 9d, 10, 15   *The Face of an Angel*
Stephen, full of grace and power, did great wonders and signs among the people. [Some] stood up and argued with Stephen. But they could not withstand the wisdom and the Spirit with which he spoke . . . And all who sat in the council . . . saw that his face was like the face of an angel.

JOHN 6:22-29   *Today's Gospel Reading*

> By faith and obedience, by constant meditation on the holiness of God, by loving righteousness and hating iniquity, by a growing acquaintance with the Spirit of holiness, we can acclimate ourselves to the fellowship of saints on earth and prepare ourselves for the eternal companionship of God and the saints above.
>
> — A. W. TOZER, *THE KNOWLEDGE OF THE HOLY*

EVENING REFLECTIONS

PSALM 9:1-2—I will give thanks to the Lord with my whole heart; I will tell of all your wonderful deeds. I will be glad and exult in you; I will sing praise to your name, O Most High.

PRAYER—Lord, let me look upon the failings of my neighbors as if they were my own, that I may be grieved with them or for them, that I may never criticize them except as love requires it, and only then with tenderness and compassion. This I pray through Christ, my Lord. Amen. **JW**

TUESDAY — WEEK 3 EASTER SEASON

PSALM 31:1-8, 14-20 ▪ ISAIAH 57:14-21 ▪ ACTS 7:51—8:1a ▪ JOHN 6:30-35

MORNING MEDITATIONS

PRAYER—O Lord, you are yourself the reason for the love wherewith we are loved. Help us to believe the intensity, the eternity of the love that has found us. Then love will cast out fear; and my troubled heart will be at peace. Amen.

PSALM 31:1-2—In you, O LORD, I seek refuge; do not let me ever be put to shame; in your righteousness deliver me. Incline your ear to me; rescue me speedily. Be a rock of refuge for me, a strong fortress to save me.

ISAIAH 57:15, 19 *I Will Heal Them*
For thus says the high and lofty one who inhabits eternity, whose name is Holy: I dwell in the high and holy place, and also with those who are contrite and humble in spirit, to revive the spirit of the humble, and to revive the heart of the contrite . . . Peace, peace, to the far and the near, says the LORD; and I will heal them.

ACTS 7:55-56 *I See the Son of Man*
But filled with the Holy Spirit, he gazed into heaven and saw the glory of God and Jesus standing at the right hand of God. "Look," he said, "I see the heavens opened and the Son of Man standing at the right hand of God!"

JOHN 6:30-35 *Today's Gospel Reading*

> As mercy is God's goodness confronting human misery and guilt, so grace is his goodness directed toward human debt and demerit. It is by his grace that God imputes merit where none previously existed and declares no debt to be where great debt had been before.
>
> A. W. TOZER, *THE KNOWLEDGE OF THE HOLY*

EVENING REFLECTIONS

PSALM 36:5, 10—Your steadfast love, O Lord, extends to the heavens, your faithfulness to the clouds . . . O continue your steadfast love to those who know you, and your salvation to the upright of heart!

PRAYER—Shepherd of Israel, I ask you to embrace me tonight with your protection. Accept my poor service today, and pardon any sinfulness displayed in my behaviors or thoughts. I pray that you will conquer sin and misery, wherever it exists, in order to hasten your kingdom. Amen. **JW**

WEDNESDAY — WEEK 3 EASTER SEASON

PSALM 66:1-12 • ISAIAH 60:1-3, 19-22 • ACTS 8:1-8 • JOHN 6:35-40

MORNING MEDITATIONS

PRAYER—Glory to you, O Jesus, who through the eternal Spirit offered yourself a full, perfect, and sufficient sacrifice for the sins of the whole world, rising the third day from the dead, and received all power both in heaven and earth. Hear my prayer. Amen. **JW**

PSALM 66:1-3a, 4-5a—Make a joyful noise to God, all the earth; sing the glory of his name; give to him glorious praise. Say to God, "How awesome are your deeds! . . . All the earth worships you; they sing praises to you, sing praises to your name." Come and see what God has done.

ISAIAH 60:19   *God Will Be Your Glory*
The sun shall no longer be your light by day, nor for brightness shall the moon give light to you by night; but the LORD will be your everlasting light, and your God will be your glory.

ACTS 8:5-6   *Philip Proclaimed the Messiah*
Philip went down to the city of Samaria and proclaimed the Messiah to them. The crowds with one accord listened eagerly to what was said by Philip, hearing and seeing the signs that he did.

JOHN 6:35-40   *Today's Gospel Reading*

> I am not ashamed of the gospel because I am not ashamed of him whom it proclaims, our Lord and Savior Jesus Christ. I am not ashamed of the fact that Christ is the Eternal Son of God, and that he who thought it not robbery to be equal with God, emptied himself and humbled himself for the salvation of the world.
>
> CLARENCE McCARTNEY, *THE GREATEST TEXTS OF THE BIBLE*

EVENING REFLECTIONS

PSALM 119:41, 44-45, 48—Let your steadfast love come to me, O LORD, your salvation according to your promise . . . I will keep your law continually, forever and ever. I shall walk at liberty, for I have sought your precepts . . . I revere your commandments, which I love.

PRAYER—Father, I know that in love for me, being lost in sin, you sent your only Son, and that he, being the Lord of Glory, humbled himself to death upon the cross so that I might be raised to glory. Accept my thanks and praise. Amen. **JW**

THURSDAY
WEEK 3 — EASTER SEASON

PSALM 66:13-20 ▪ ISAIAH 61 ▪ ACTS 8:26-40 ▪ JOHN 6:44-51

MORNING MEDITATIONS

PRAYER—Father, bless all those who have been helpful to me throughout my life by their assistance, advice, and example. Bless all those who do not, or cannot pray for themselves. Change the hearts of my enemies and give me grace to forgive them, even as you for Christ's sake have forgiven me. Amen. **JW**

PSALM 66:16, 19-20—Come and hear, all you who fear God, and I will tell what he has done for me . . . Truly God has listened; he has given heed to the words of my prayer. Blessed be God, because he has not rejected my prayer or removed his steadfast love from me.

ISAIAH 61:10abc *He Has Clothed Me*
I will greatly rejoice in the Lord, my whole being shall exult in my God; for he has clothed me with the garments of salvation, he has covered me with the robe of righteousness.

ACTS 8:29-30a, 30c-31a, 35 *The Good News About Jesus*
Then the Spirit said to Philip, "Go over to this chariot and join it." So Philip ran up to it . . . He asked, "Do you understand what you are reading?" He replied, "How can I, unless someone guides me?" . . . Then Philip began to speak, and . . . proclaimed to him the good news about Jesus.

JOHN 6:44-51 *Today's Gospel Reading*

> I am not ashamed of the great miracle by which Christ came into the world, that the eternal Son of God became man by taking to himself a body and a reasoning soul, being conceived by the power of the Holy Spirit in the womb of the Virgin Mary and born of her, yet without sin. —CLARENCE McCARTNEY, *THE GREATEST TEXTS OF THE BIBLE*

EVENING REFLECTIONS

PSALM 37:27-28, 34—Depart from evil, and do good; so you shall abide forever. For the Lord loves justice; he will not forsake his faithful ones . . . Wait for the Lord, and keep to his way, and he will exalt you to inherit the land.

PRAYER—O Lord our Lord, there is none like you in heaven above or in the earth beneath. Yours is the greatness and the dignity and the majesty. All that is in the heaven and on the earth is yours. To you belong the kingdom and the power and the glory forever, O God. Amen.

FRIDAY — WEEK 3 EASTER SEASON

PSALM 117 • ISAIAH 63:7-19 • ACTS 9:1-20 • JOHN 6:52-59

MORNING MEDITATIONS

PRAYER—Almighty God, I bless you from my heart. O Savior of the World, God of God, Light of Light, you have destroyed the power of the devil, you have overcome death, and you sit at the right hand of the Father. Be today my light and peace, and make me a new creature, through Christ my Lord. Amen. **JW**

PSALM 117—Praise the Lord, all you nations! Extol him, all you peoples! For great is his steadfast love toward us, and the faithfulness of the Lord endures forever. Praise the Lord!

ISAIAH 63:7   God's Mercy Remembered
I will recount the gracious deeds of the Lord, the praiseworthy acts of the Lord, because of all that the Lord has done for us and the great favor to the house of Israel that he has shown them according to his mercy, according to the abundance of his steadfast love.

ACTS 9:19b-20   Jesus Is the Son of God
For several days [Paul] was with the disciples in Damascus, and immediately he began to proclaim Jesus in the synagogues, saying, "He is the Son of God."

JOHN 6:52-59   Today's Gospel Reading

> I am not ashamed of the miracles of Christ. If you get rid of the miracles you get rid of Christ, for the only Christ we know is the one who worked great miracles . . . I am not ashamed of the fact that they certify to his divine power and prove, as he himself said, "that the Son of man has power on earth to forgive sins."
>
> CLARENCE McCARTNEY, *THE GREATEST TEXTS OF THE BIBLE*

EVENING REFLECTIONS

PSALM 105:42a, 43, 45—He remembered his holy promise . . . So he brought his people out with joy, his chosen ones with singing . . . that they might keep his statutes and observe his laws. Praise the Lord!

PRAYER—O God, be gracious to all who are near and dear to me. You know their names and their needs. In your goodness, bless them according to those needs through Jesus Christ my Lord. Amen. **JW**

SATURDAY
WEEK 3 — EASTER SEASON

PSALM 116:12-19 • ISAIAH 65:17-25 • ACTS 9:28-42 • JOHN 6:60-69

MORNING MEDITATIONS

PRAYER—O God, my Savior, my Sanctifier, keep your face turned toward me. Kindle within me the desires to confirm and increase my faith, and fulfill your plans for me. Amen. *JW*

PSALM 116:12-14—What shall I return to the LORD for all his bounty to me? I will lift up the cup of salvation and call on the name of the LORD. I will pay my vows to the LORD in the presence of his people.

ISAIAH 65:17-18a   *Rejoice Forever in What I Am Creating*
For I am about to create new heavens and a new earth; the former things shall not be remembered or come to mind. But be glad and rejoice forever in what I am creating.

ACTS 9:28, 31   *Speaking Boldly in the Name of the Lord*
So [Paul] went in and out among them in Jerusalem, speaking boldly in the name of the Lord . . . Meanwhile the church throughout Judea, Galilee, and Samaria had peace and was built up. Living in the fear of the Lord and in the comfort of the Holy Spirit, it increased in numbers.

JOHN 6:60-69   *Today's Gospel Reading*

> I am not ashamed of Christ as a friend. What a wonderful friend he is! I am ashamed of the fact that so often I have been unworthy of his friendship and faithless to him. But of him I am not ashamed.
> — CLARENCE McCARTNEY, *THE GREATEST TEXTS OF THE BIBLE*

EVENING REFLECTIONS

PSALM 43:3-4a—O send out your light and your truth; let them lead me; let them bring me to your holy hill and to your dwelling. Then I will go to the altar of God, to God my exceeding joy.

PRAYER—Lord God, you have left us your holy word to be a lantern to our feet and a light unto our steps. Give us your Holy Spirit that out of the same word we may learn what your eternal will is and frame our lives in holy obedience to it, through Jesus Christ our Lord. Amen. *JW*

WEEK FOUR
Easter Season

Ashes to Fire Week 10

Sunday: Tell Us Plainly

Read the gospel passage from John 10:22-30 and the devotional reflection titled "Tell Us Plainly," then respond to the discussion prompts in the Reflective Journaling section.

THE MUSIC OF ASHES TO FIRE

Week 10: "Do This in Me" (Track 11)

Monday through Saturday

IN THE MORNING:

A personal daily devotional guide includes prayer, a reading from the Old Testament, the Psalms, the Epistles, and the Gospels for each day of the week.

In addition to the daily psalm, this week's readings come from Zechariah, the Acts of the Apostles, and the gospel of John.

Inspirational quotes from men and women of faith keep us in contact with our shared Christian heritage.

IN THE EVENING:

An evening psalm and prayer become preludes to nighttime rest and renewal.

Easter Season—Week Four
Tell Us Plainly

SUNDAY

A devotional reflection based on John 10:22-30

Read the gospel passage first, then the devotional reflection that follows. The discussion prompts at the end will help prepare you for Sunday school and small-group sessions.

I've started reading poetry this year, but that's not the sort of thing you say in public, because no matter who is around, you're going to end up looking pretty dumb. Maybe your friends will think that because you've recently gotten into this poetry stuff, you are turning sentimental and romantic on them. They'll expect you to quit your job any day now in order to take up permanent residence in a coffee shop, which is of course where all poetry readers are when they aren't up in the clouds.

For fear of these reactions I didn't tell anyone when I started to pick up books of poetry here and there. I just spent a lot of time in my tiny room reading out loud to myself. They say that's the only way to read poetry—out loud. That's so your mouth can set down the words in a more tangible way, as if you were speaking reality into existence. But I found it awkward, forming my lips around words I didn't understand and listening to their foreign sounds buzzing in my head. It was uncomfortable sitting with meanings that weren't self-evident and learning to let incomplete thoughts hang in the air long after I was finished reading. Slowly but surely, however, there was a shift, and I began enjoying the richness of spoken mystery. In fact, the mystery became powerful; it was what I most looked forward to. I was starting to get it. Or rather, I was starting to get that I didn't get it, and that getting it was never the point. That instead, the poetry was getting me, reading me, and discerning me somehow.

John 10 takes place during the winterish months at the time of a Jewish celebration called the Festival of the Dedication or Festival of the Lights. Knowing this won't change your perception of the passage unless you understand its origin, understand, for example, that this festival probably more than any other contained an atmosphere of heroism and triumphalism and a longing for more of both. It was at this time every year that the people celebrated Judas Maccabaeus, a man famous for defeating the Seleucid king who tried to abolish Judaism in 170 BC. The Seleucid king was serious trouble; before Maccabaeus was able to successfully lead a revolt against him, this king had killed more than eighty thousand Jews, crucified mothers who circumcised their children, and turned the temple into an altar for the pagan god Zeus. This victory against the Seleucids served as such a meaningful example of God's salvation that the Jews set aside eight days every year to remember it.

It is with this sort of Maccabean expectation that Jesus is approached by the Jewish leaders of the day with the question, "How long will you keep us in suspense? If you are the Messiah, tell us plainly" (v. 24). Or in other words, "If you want us to believe you, show us something great!" We must keep in mind that so far Jesus' ministry has seemed strange and small. Just prior to this passage Jesus was describing his authority using a shepherd metaphor (vv. 1-16). And before that, he was telling some confusing parables and performing a small number of healings on people who were nearby or just kind of around—persons he passed on the street, a couple of friends, a random woman grabbing at his coat. Certainly this wasn't the political story of salvation and glory the people were hoping for.

In response to their demand for new information, Jesus only extends his earlier shepherd metaphor: "I have told you, and you do not believe. The works that I do in my Father's name testify to me; but you do not believe, because you do not belong to my sheep. My sheep hear my voice. I know them, and they follow me" (vv. 25-27).

As an aside, because I have grown used to Scripture, I come to the text with certain predispositions. For instance, I know that whenever religious leaders approach Jesus, they are generally up to no good. I know also I should feel reaffirmed because I am not like them. I know further I should feel good about the fact that I am a sheep—without a doubt a sheep—that my "sheepness" is so "sheepy" and my coat so woolly that I am practically walking insulation. Yes, I think, I *should* feel these things—but I don't. When I encounter this passage, I instead find myself feeling more like the Jewish leaders. I hear myself saying, "Me too" and "Tell us plainly." "Tell us plainly," I ask of him when things are winterish and when I'm facing the king of the Seleucids, when I'm suffering a prolonged illness, unemployed, and despairing. "Tell us plainly," I ask before things even get that desperate. "Tell us plainly," I ask all too easily when I am missing the point—which is belief.

For the record, I don't think God is scared of our asking things. A friend of mine says, "What more audacious thing can we do than ask God for his Son's body in Holy Communion?" But that's exactly it, he—God—is enough. Believing that Christ came so we could be united with him and his Father forever is all the "plain speak" necessary for salvation—and still, isn't it terribly mysterious? Even belief must be given to us. "I give them eternal life, and they will never perish. No one will snatch them out of my hand. What my Father has given me is greater than all else, and no one can snatch it out of the Father's hand. The Father and I are one" (vv. 28-30).

Where miracles and signs are powerless to change the human heart, God gives us instead Christ the Word—powerful and effective to keep us, yet terribly inscrutable and other.

So have mercy on us when we don't always understand, Lord; it's just that we're still learning how to read poetry. —Elizabeth Perry

After reading the passage from John 10:22-30 and the devotional reflection "Tell Us Plainly," you may also want to read the following related passages:
Acts 9:36-43; Psalm 23; Revelation 7:9-17

The discussion prompts that follow will help prepare you to participate in your Sunday school class or small-group study. Use your Reflective Journaling section to record any other insights that come to you as you read the gospel lesson and the devotional reflection.

DISCUSSION PROMPT NO. 1: JOHN 10:22-30
Why do you think those who were listening to Jesus in the temple were unable to understand his answer to their question, "Are you the Messiah?" (see v. 24).

DISCUSSION PROMPT NO. 2: JOHN 10:22-30
What characteristics does Jesus cite for those he identifies as "my sheep" (v. 26)?

DISCUSSION PROMPT NO. 3: JOHN 10:22-30
What promises does Jesus make to his sheep?

DISCUSSION PROMPT NO. 4: JOHN 10:22-30
In what ways do you think Jesus and the Father are one?

DISCUSSION PROMPT NO. 5: DEVOTIONAL REFLECTION
What do you think the writer means with her comment, "For the record, I don't think God is scared of our asking things"?

Reflective Journaling

MONDAY | WEEK 4 EASTER SEASON

PSALM 42:1-7 ▪ ZECHARIAH 6:15—7:7 ▪ ACTS 11:1-18 ▪ JOHN 10:1-10

MORNING MEDITATIONS

PRAYER—Lord Jesus, let me know myself and know you, and desire nothing save only you. Let me hate myself and love you. Let me do everything for the sake of you. Let me humble myself and exalt you. Let me think of nothing except you. Let me die to myself and live in you. Amen. ***St. Augustine***

PSALM 42:1-2a, 5-6a—As the deer longs for flowing streams, so my soul longs for you, O God. My soul thirsts for God . . . Why are you cast down, O my soul, and why are you disquieted within me? Hope in God; for I shall again praise him, my help and my God.

ZECHARIAH 6:15 *The Lord of Hosts Has Sent Me*
Those who are far off shall come and help to build the temple of the Lord; and you shall know that the Lord of hosts has sent me to you. This will happen if you diligently obey the voice of the Lord your God.

ACTS 11:15-16 *Baptized with the Holy Spirit*
As I began to speak, the Holy Spirit fell upon them just as it had upon us at the beginning. And I remembered the word of the Lord, how he had said, "John baptized with water, but you will be baptized with the Holy Spirit."

JOHN 10:1-10 *Today's Gospel Reading*

> What sort of garland did Christ Jesus . . . submit to on behalf of humanity? One made of thorns and thistles—a symbol of our sins, produced by the soil of the flesh. However, the power of the cross removed these thorns, blunting death's every sting in the Lord's enduring head. ***TERTULLIAN, CHAPLET 14***

EVENING REFLECTIONS

PSALM 41:10a, 12-13—But you, O Lord, be gracious to me, and raise me up . . . But you have upheld me because of my integrity, and set me in your presence forever. Blessed be the Lord, the God of Israel, from everlasting to everlasting. Amen and Amen.

PRAYER—Lord Jesus, let me accept whatever happens as from you. Let me banish self and follow you, and ever desire to follow you. Let me fly from myself and take refuge in you, that I may deserve to be defended by you. Let me fear for myself. Let me fear you, and let me be among those who are chosen by you. Amen. ***St. Augustine***

TUESDAY
WEEK 4 — EASTER SEASON

PSALM 87:1-7 ▪ ZECHARIAH 7:8-14 ▪ ACTS 11:19-26 ▪ JOHN 10:11-18

MORNING MEDITATIONS

PRAYER—Great are you, O Lord, and greatly to be praised; man desires to praise you, for he is a part of your creation; he bears his mortality about with him and carries the evidence of his sin and the proof that you resist the proud Still you desire that he should delight to praise you, for you have made us for yourself and our hearts are restless until they come to rest in you. **St. Augustine**

PSALM 87:1-2—On the holy mount stands the city he founded; the LORD loves the gates of Zion more than all the dwellings of Jacob. Glorious things are spoken of you, O city of God.

ZECHARIAH 7:9-10 *Show Kindness and Mercy*
Render true judgments, show kindness and mercy to one another; do not oppress the widow, the orphan, the alien, or the poor; and do not devise evil in your hearts against one another.

ACTS 11:23-24 *A Good Man Full of Faith*
When [Barnabas] came and saw the grace of God, he rejoiced, and he exhorted them all to remain faithful to the Lord with steadfast devotion; for he was a good man, full of the Holy Spirit and of faith. And a great many people were brought to the Lord.

JOHN 10:11-18 *Today's Gospel Reading*

> This is the will of God which Christ did and taught: humility in conversation; steadfastness in faith; modesty in words; justice in deeds; mercy in works; discipline in morals; inability to do a wrong and ability to bear a wrong done; to keep peace with the brothers and sisters.   ST. CYPRIAN, *TREATISE* 4, PARAS. 14-15

EVENING REFLECTIONS

PSALM 48:9-10, 1—We ponder your steadfast love, O God, in the midst of your temple. Your name, O God, like your praise, reaches to the ends of the earth. Your right hand is filled with victory . . . Great is the LORD and greatly to be praised.

PRAYER—Lord Jesus, let me be willing to obey for the sake of you. Let me cling to nothing save only to you, and let me serve the poor because of you. Look upon me, that I may love you. Call me that I may see you, and forever enjoy you. Amen. **St. Augustine**

WEDNESDAY
WEEK 4 EASTER SEASON

PSALM 67:1-8 • ZECHARIAH 8:1-8 • ACTS 12:24—13:5 • JOHN 12:44-50

MORNING MEDITATIONS

PRAYER—Lord God, send your Holy Spirit to be the guide of all my ways and the sanctifier of my soul and body. Give me the light of your presence, your peace from heaven, and the salvation of my soul, through Jesus Christ my Lord. Amen. *JW*

PSALM 67:1-2, 7—May God be gracious to us and bless us and make his face to shine upon us, that your way may be known upon earth, your saving power among all nations . . . May God continue to bless us; let all the ends of the earth revere him.

ZECHARIAH 8:3, 8b   *They Shall Be My People*
Thus says the LORD: I will return to Zion, and will dwell in the midst of Jerusalem; Jerusalem shall be called the faithful city . . . They shall be my people and I will be their God, in faithfulness and in righteousness.

ACTS 13:1a, 2-3   *They Laid Their Hands on Them*
Now in the church at Antioch there were prophets and teachers . . . While they were worshiping the Lord and fasting, the Holy Spirit said, "Set apart for me Barnabas and Saul for the work to which I have called them." Then after fasting and praying they laid their hands on them and sent them off.

JOHN 12:44-50   *Today's Gospel Reading*

> This is the will of God which Christ both did and taught . . . to love God with all our hearts; to love Him as a Father; to fear Him as God; to prefer nothing above Christ (because He did not prefer anything above us); to adhere inseparable to his love; to stand by his cross bravely and faithfully.
>
> ST. CYPRIAN, *TREATISE 4*, PARAS. 14-15

EVENING REFLECTIONS

PSALM 49:7-8, 15a—No ransom avails for one's life, there is no price one can give to God for it. For the ransom of life is costly, and can never suffice . . . But God will ransom my soul.

PRAYER—Watch, O Lord, with those who wake, or watch, or weep tonight, and give your angels charge over those who sleep. Tend your sick ones, O Lord Christ. Rest your weary ones. Bless your dying ones. Soothe your suffering ones. Pity your afflicted ones. Shield your joyous ones. And for all your love's sake. Amen. **St. Augustine**

THURSDAY
WEEK 4 — EASTER SEASON

PSALM 89:1-18 ▪ ZECHARIAH 8:9-17 ▪ ACTS 13:13-25 ▪ JOHN 13:16-20

MORNING MEDITATIONS

PRAYER—My God, let me know and love you, so that I may find my happiness in you. Enable me to know you ever more on earth, so that I may know you perfectly in heaven. Enable me to love you ever more on earth, so that I may love you perfectly in heaven. In that way my joy may be great on earth, and perfect with you in heaven. Amen. **St. Augustine**

PSALM 89:1-2—I will sing of your steadfast love, O Lord, forever; with my mouth I will proclaim your faithfulness to all generations. I declare that your steadfast love is established forever; your faithfulness is as firm as the heavens.

ZECHARIAH 8:12, 13b   Let Your Hands Be Strong
There shall be a sowing of peace; the vine shall yield its fruit, the ground shall give its produce, and the skies shall give their dew; and I will cause a remnant of this people to possess all these things . . . Do not be afraid, but let your hands be strong.

ACTS 13:22b-23   God Has Brought a Savior to Israel
In [the Lord's] testimony about [David] he said, "I have found David, son of Jesse, to be a man after my heart, who will carry out all my wishes!" Of this man's posterity God has brought to Israel a Savior, Jesus, as he promised.

JOHN 13:16-20   Today's Gospel Reading

> Throughout this time between the Lord's resurrection and ascension, the Lord in his providence fulfilled one purpose, taught one lesson, set one consideration before the eyes and hearts of his followers: that the Lord Jesus Christ, who was truly born, truly suffered and truly died, should be recognized as truly risen.
>
> ST. LEO THE GREAT, *SERMON 1 ON THE ASCENSION*

EVENING REFLECTIONS

PSALM 113:1-3—Praise the Lord! Praise, O servants of the Lord; praise the name of the Lord. Blessed be the name of the Lord from this time on and forevermore. From the rising of the sun to its setting the name of the Lord is to be praised.

PRAYER—O my God, I love you above all things, with my whole heart and soul, because you are worthy of all my love. I forgive all who have injured me, and I ask pardon for all whom I may have injured. Amen. **JW**

FRIDAY
WEEK 4 — EASTER SEASON

PSALM 2 • ZECHARIAH 8:18-23 • ACTS 13:26-33 • JOHN 14:1-6

MORNING MEDITATIONS

PRAYER—Almighty God, I bless you from my heart. O Savior of the World, God of God, Light of Light, you have destroyed the power of the devil, you have overcome death, and you sit at the right hand of the Father. Be today my light and peace and make me a new creature, through Christ my Lord. Amen. *JW*

PSALM 2:7-8a, 11, 13c—I will tell of the decree of the Lord: he said to me, "You are my son; today I have begotten you. Ask of me, and I will make the nations your heritage" . . . Serve the Lord with fear, with trembling . . . Happy are all who take refuge in him.

ZECHARIAH 8:21b, 22, 23c *We Have Heard That God Is with You*
"Come, let us go to entreat the favor of the Lord, and to seek the Lord of hosts" . . . Many peoples and strong nations shall come to seek the Lord of hosts in Jerusalem, and to entreat the favor of the Lord . . . "Let us go with you, for we have heard that God is with you."

ACTS 13:32-33 *We Bring Good News*
We bring you the good news that what God promised to our ancestors he has fulfilled for us, their children, by raising Jesus; as also it is written in the second psalm, "You are my Son; today I have begotten you."

JOHN 14:1-6 *Today's Gospel Reading*

> Who can describe the blessed bond of the love of God? Who is able to tell the excellence of its beauty as it ought to be told? Love unites us to God . . . Let us pray and implore of his mercy, that we may live blameless in love, free from all human partialities for one above another.
> ST. CLEMENT, *I CLEMENT* 49-50

EVENING REFLECTIONS

PSALM 40:1-3a—I waited patiently for the Lord; he inclined to me and heard my cry. He drew me up from the desolate pit, out of the miry bog, and set my feet upon a rock, making my steps secure. He put a new song in my mouth, a song of praise to our God.

PRAYER—O God of truth, grant me the happiness of heaven so that my joy may fulfill your promise. In the meantime let my mind dwell on that happiness, my tongue speak of it, my heart pine for it, my mouth pronounce it, my soul hunger for it, my flesh thirst for it, and my entire being desire it until I enter through death in the joy of my Lord forever. Amen.
St. Augustine

SATURDAY
WEEK 4 — EASTER SEASON

PSALM 98:1-4 ▪ ZECHARIAH 9:1-8 ▪ ACTS 13:44-52 ▪ JOHN 14:7-14

MORNING MEDITATIONS

PRAYER—For your mercies' sake, O Lord my God, tell me what you are to me. Say to my soul: "I am your salvation." So speak that I may hear, O Lord; my heart is listening; open it that it may hear you, and say to my soul: "I am your salvation." After hearing this word, may you . . . cleanse me, O Lord. Amen. **St. Augustine**

PSALM 98:1, 4—Sing to the Lord a new song, for he has done marvelous things. His right hand and his holy arm have gotten him victory . . . Make a joyful noise to the Lord . . . break forth into joyous song and sing praises.

ZECHARIAH 9:6b, 8   *The Return of the Divine Warrior*
I will make an end of the pride of Philistia . . . I will encamp at my house as a guard, so that no one shall march to and fro; no oppressor shall again overrun them, for now I have seen with my own eyes.

ACTS 13:47-48   *A Light to the Gentiles*
The Lord has commanded us, saying, "I have set you to be a light for the Gentiles, so that you may bring salvation to the ends of the earth." When the Gentiles heard this, they were glad and praised the word of the Lord; and as many as had been destined for eternal life became believers.

JOHN 14:7-14   *Today's Gospel Reading*

> Because Christ wished to show his disciples how necessary it is to be rooted in love of him . . . he told them in figurative language that he was the vine, and that the branches of the vine were those who were united with him . . . By the gift of the Spirit they are united with him by faith and every kind of holiness.   ST. CYRIL OF ALEXANDRIA, *COMMENTARY ON JOHN*

EVENING REFLECTIONS

PSALM 55:22—Cast your burden on the Lord, and he will sustain you; he will never permit the righteous to be moved.

PRAYER—God of life, there are days when the burdens we carry chafe our shoulders and wear us down; when the road seems dreary and endless, the skies gray and threatening; when our lives have no music in them and our hearts are lonely, and our souls have lost their courage. Flood the path with light, and turn our eyes to where the skies are full of promise. Amen. **St. Augustine**

WEEK FIVE
*E*ASTER *S*EASON

Ashes to Fire Week 11

Sunday: The New Commandment

Read the gospel passage from John 13:31-35 and the devotional reflection titled "The New Commandment," then respond to the discussion prompts in the Reflective Journaling section.

THE MUSIC OF ASHES TO FIRE

Week 11: "Love As You Have Loved" (Track 12)

Monday through Saturday

IN THE MORNING:

A personal daily devotional guide includes prayer, a reading from the Old Testament, the Psalms, the Epistles, and the Gospels for each day of the week.

In addition to the daily psalm, this week's readings come from Zechariah, the Acts of the Apostles, and the gospel of John.

Inspirational quotes from men and women of faith keep us in contact with our shared Christian heritage.

IN THE EVENING:

An evening psalm and prayer become preludes to nighttime rest and renewal.

SUNDAY

Easter Season—Week Five
The New Commandment

A devotional reflection based on John 13:31-35

Read the gospel passage first, then the devotional reflection that follows. The discussion prompts at the end will help prepare you for Sunday school and small-group sessions.

The time remaining with Jesus' disciples slipped quickly away. Jesus was more aware that the precious moments were passing than were the disciples. When his disciples later realized this had been his last evening of earthly ministry with them, they went back in their minds and stitched together what he had said. No doubt, Jesus used that evening to give them last-minute instructions of the most important kind; they were things he wanted them to remember. People still do the same thing today, imparting important messages to loved ones just before leaving this earth. So what did Jesus consider most important in those closing hours? What did he want to make sure they recalled after he returned to his Father?

As the disciples recalled their last evening together with Jesus, they remembered that his tone changed as soon as Judas left them. Jesus spoke as though he had already begun his journey to the cross. His love for his Father and for his disciples, throughout all time, kept his mind firmly fixed on the necessity of making that journey. It was as though his eyes had already looked into the hours ahead at the trouble that awaited him. But he also seemed to see beyond the trouble to a glorious victory just on the other side.

Neither Jesus' disciples long ago nor we today can comprehend how the great God of the universe could be glorified by the human suffering of his Son on a cross (John 13:31-32). Those words seem strange to us. The Father glorified in his Son's obedience and suffering? However, in a way known only to God, the weakness of the cross became the power of God for the redemption of humanity. Jesus was lifted up to divine glory and exalted by God in ways Jesus' enemies never intended by their cruel actions. They meant to bring him harm, but in a strange turn of events, God turned their intentions on their heads and brought about great good by glorifying his Son. God often links suffering and glory together in ways we have difficulty understanding (e.g., 1 Pet. 1:11).

Jesus used that last evening with his disciples to call them a special name, as recounted John 13:33. He only referred to his disciples as "little children" this one time in the Gospels. He considered it an affectionate name. He loved them very much and wanted to remind them of his tender love for them before he left them that evening—their last night together. They hoped their days of ministry with Jesus remained unnumbered, but not so. His time of departure had arrived; his ministry on earth was complete. He left them his ministry to carry on after his departure.

Jesus left his disciples with a powerful new command: "Love one another" (v. 34). What is so new about this command? Does this command not summarize the Old Testament command to love God and your neighbor (Matt. 22:38-39)? We know we must love God with all our heart, soul, and mind, but how does the Old Testament tell us to love others? "As yourself," it says. The Old Testament assumed you loved yourself and cared for your own physical, emotional, social, psychological, and spiritual needs. You should love others accordingly.

Jesus shifted the Old Testament motivation from self-regard to "as I have loved you" (John 13:34). How did Jesus love us? His love for us caused him to sacrifice himself for us, to abandon himself for us, to put others first, to claim no rights for himself, and to ultimately die on the cross for all humanity. As Paul reminded us in Phil. 2:7-8, "[He] emptied himself, taking the form of a slave, being born in human likeness. And being found in human form, he humbled himself and became obedient to the point of death—even death on a cross."

These last words of Jesus set forth a blueprint to give his disciples a unique mark in the world. "Everyone will know that you are my disciples, if . . . ," he said (John 13:35). Jesus knew it is not the normal reaction of people to respond in such loving ways when provoked or mistreated. Jesus knew it is not the normal reaction of human nature to respond in such self-sacrificing ways when attacked by enemies. Jesus knew it is not the normal reaction of disciples to respond in such self-abandoning ways when a miscarriage of justice blamed the innocent.

Jesus was a master teacher with his disciples that last night, not because he closed the evening with powerful last words, but because he left them with a powerful challenge. He then did something far more instructional. He actually put those words into action by living them out before his disciples. They saw his life as an object lesson illustrating the very love he so desperately wanted them to embody. He walked out of the upper room that night and headed straight for the cross.

The new commandment: "As I have loved you, you also should love one another" (v. 34). —Frank Moore

After reading the passage from John 13:31-35 and the devotional reflection "The New Commandment," you may also want to read the following related passages:

Acts 11:1-18; Psalm 148; Revelation 21:1-6

The discussion prompts that follow will help prepare you to participate in your Sunday school class or small-group study. Use your Reflective Journaling section to record any other insights that come to you as you read the gospel lesson and the devotional reflection.

DISCUSSION PROMPT NO. 1: JOHN 13:31-35
In what ways did Jesus glorify God?

DISCUSSION PROMPT NO. 2: JOHN 13:31-35
Jesus' knowledge of his limited time of earthly ministry gave urgency to his mission. Since we all have a limited number of days of mortal life, how should that fact impact our priorities and the service we offer in Christ's name?

DISCUSSION PROMPT NO. 3: JOHN 13:31-35
What do you think Jesus meant when he said, "Where I am going, you cannot come" (v. 33)?

DISCUSSION PROMPT NO. 4: JOHN 13:31-35
What is the quality and the impact of the love that Jesus commands of his disciples?

DISCUSSION PROMPT NO. 5: DEVOTIONAL REFLECTION
Do you find these words of Jesus comforting? Explain.

Reflective Journaling

MONDAY | WEEK 5 EASTER SEASON

PSALM 115:1-4, 15-16 ▪ ZECHARIAH 9:9-13 ▪ ACTS 14:5-18 ▪ JOHN 14:21-26

MORNING MEDITATIONS

PRAYER—Breathe in me, O Holy Spirit, that my thoughts may all be holy. Act in me, O Holy Spirit, that my work, too, may be holy. Draw my heart, O Holy Spirit, that I love but what is holy. Strengthen me, O Holy Spirit, to defend all that is holy. Guard me, then, O Holy Spirit, that I always may be holy. Amen. **St. Augustine**

PSALM 115:1, 16—Not to us, O Lord, not to us, but to your name give glory; for the sake of your steadfast love and your faithfulness . . . The heavens are the Lord's, but the earth he has given to human beings . . . But we will bless the Lord, from this time on and forevermore. Praise the Lord!

ZECHARIAH 9:9a-c, 10c-e   *Your King Comes*
Rejoice greatly, O daughter Zion! Shout aloud, O daughter Jerusalem! Lo, your king comes to you; triumphant and victorious is he . . . and he shall command peace to the nations; his dominion shall be from sea to sea, and from the River to the ends of the earth.

ACTS 14:15   *Turn to God*
Friends . . . we are mortals just like you, and we bring you good news, that you should turn from these worthless things to the living God, who made the heaven and the earth.

JOHN 14:21-26   *Today's Gospel Reading*

As the sun naturally shines, as the day gives light, as the fountain flows, as the rain produces moisture, so does the heavenly Spirit instill himself into us. When the soul, in its gaze into heaven, has recognized its Author . . . it begins to be that which it believes itself to be. ST. CYPRIAN, *EPISTLE 1*, PARA. 14

EVENING REFLECTIONS

PSALM 57:1-2, 5—Be merciful to me, O God, be merciful to me, for in you my soul takes refuge; in the shadow of your wings I will take refuge, until the destroying storms pass by. I cry to God Most High, the God who fulfills he purpose for me . . . Be exalted, O God, above the heavens. Let your glory be over all the earth.

PRAYER—Gracious Holy Spirit, look with mercy on all those who suffer affliction. Hear the cries of the sick, the oppressed, the imprisoned, the poor and needy. Give to my enemies grace and pardon. Enable me to love them, to bless those who curse me, to do good to those who despise me, and to pray for those who mistreat me. Amen. **JW**

TUESDAY
WEEK 5 EASTER SEASON

PSALM 145:10-21 ▪ ZECHARIAH 9:14-17 ▪ ACTS 14:19-28 ▪ JOHN 14:27-31

MORNING MEDITATIONS

PRAYER—In your mercy, O God, accept my morning sacrifice of praise and thanksgiving. I offer it up to you with a full heart. You are praised by all your works. Amidst the jubilation of nature, do not let your human family remain silent. Let those of us who are your children offer the noblest praise. Amen. ***JW***

PSALM 145:10-11, 17-18—All your works shall give thanks to you, O LORD, and all your faithful shall bless you. They shall speak of the glory of your kingdom, and tell of your power . . . The LORD is just in all his ways, and kind in all his doings. The LORD is near to all who call on him, to all who call on him in truth.

ZECHARIAH 9:16-17a *God Will Save Them*
On that day the LORD their God will save them for they are the flock of his people; for like the jewels of a crown they shall shine on his land. For what goodness and beauty are his!

ACTS 14:21-22 *Through Many Persecutions*
After they had proclaimed the good news to that city and had made many disciples, they . . . [went on] to Iconium and Antioch. There they strengthened the souls of the disciples and encouraged them to continue in the faith, saying, "It is through many persecutions that we must enter the kingdom of God."

JOHN 14:27-31 *Today's Gospel Reading*

> While Jesus was with his disciples visibly, he could not belong to all the world. While he was ministering to the needy folk of Galilee, he could not be equally the possession of humankind . . . Only by departing from the vision of the privileged few could he reign by his Spirit in the hearts of all.
>
> JAMES STEWART, *THE STRONG NAME*

EVENING REFLECTIONS

PSALM 62:1-2, 12a—For God alone my soul waits in silence; from him comes my salvation. He alone is my rock and my salvation, my fortress; I shall never be shaken . . . Steadfast love belongs to you, O Lord.

PRAYER—Give me yourself, O my God . . . Behold I love you, and if my love is too weak a thing, grant me to love you more strongly. I cannot measure my love to know how much it falls short . . . but let my soul hasten to your embrace and never be turned away until it is hidden in the secret shelter of your presence. Amen. ***St. Augustine***

WEDNESDAY
WEEK 5 — EASTER SEASON

PSALM 122:1-9 ▪ ZECHARIAH 10:1-7 ▪ ACTS 15:1-11 ▪ JOHN 15:1-8

MORNING MEDITATIONS

PRAYER—O my God, this only do I know, that it is not good for me when you are not with me, when you are only outside me. I want you in my very self. All the plenty in the world which is not my God is utter want. Amen. **St. Augustine**

PSALM 122:1, 6-7, 9b—I was glad when they said to me, "Let us go to the house of the LORD!" . . . Pray for the peace of Jerusalem: "May they prosper who love you. Peace be within your walls, and security within your towers" . . . I will seek your good.

ZECHARIAH 10:6 *I Will Answer Them*
I will strengthen the house of Judah, and I will save the house of Joseph. I will bring them back because I have compassion on them, and they shall be as though I had not rejected them; for I am the LORD their God and I will answer them.

ACTS 15:8-9 *Hearts Cleansed by Faith*
And God, who knows the human heart, testified to them by giving them the Holy Spirit, as he did to us; and in cleansing their hearts by faith he has made no distinction between them and us.

JOHN 15:1-8 *Today's Gospel Reading*

> As I well remember, the atheist too has his moments of shuddering misgiving, of an all but irresistible suspicion that old tales may after all be true, that something or someone from outside may at any moment break into his neat, explicable, mechanical universe.
>
> C. S. LEWIS, *CHRISTIAN REFLECTIONS*

EVENING REFLECTIONS

PSALM 119:89-90, 93—The LORD exists forever; your word is firmly fixed in heaven. Your faithfulness endures to all generations; you have established the earth, and it stands fast . . . I will never forget your precepts, for by them you have given me life.

PRAYER—Lord and Savior, you are the way, the truth and the life. You have said that we cannot follow you unless we renounce ourselves. I know, my Savior, that you place no requirement upon us that we cannot bear with the assistance of your grace. May I seek only your will in all things. Amen. **JW**

THURSDAY
WEEK 5 EASTER SEASON

PSALM 96:1-10 ▪ ZECHARIAH 10:8-12 ▪ ACTS 15:12-21 ▪ JOHN 15:9-11

MORNING MEDITATIONS

PRAYER—Eternal God, my Sovereign Lord, watch over me today with eyes of mercy, direct my soul and body according to your will, and fill my heart with your Holy Spirit that I may live this day, and all the rest of my days, to your glory. Amen. *JW*

PSALM 96:6-7, 9—Honor and majesty are before him; strength and beauty are in his sanctuary. Ascribe to the LORD, O families of the peoples, ascribe to the LORD glory and strength . . . Worship the LORD in holy splendor; tremble before him, all the earth.

ZECHARIAH 10:8, 10a, 12 *I Have Redeemed Them*
I will signal for them and gather them in, for I have redeemed them, and they shall be as numerous as they were before . . . I will bring them home . . . I will make them strong in the LORD, and they shall walk in his name, says the LORD.

ACTS 15:13a, 15-17 *The Gentiles Will Seek the Lord*
James replied, "My brothers . . . this agrees with the words of the prophets, as it is written, 'After this I will return, and I will rebuild the dwelling of David, which has fallen . . . and I will set it up, so that all other peoples may seek the Lord—even all the Gentiles over whom my name has been called.'"

JOHN 15:9-11 *Today's Gospel Reading*

> [Jesus] warned people to "count the cost" before becoming Christians. "Make no mistake," He says, "if you let Me, I will make you perfect. The moment you put yourself into My hands, that is what you are in for. Nothing less, or other, than that.
>
> C. S. LEWIS, *MERE CHRISTIANITY*

EVENING REFLECTIONS

PSALM 71:17, 21-22a, 23-24a—O God, from my youth you have taught me, and I still proclaim your wondrous deeds . . . You will increase my honor, and comfort me once again. I will also praise you . . . My lips will shout for joy when I sing praises to you; my soul also, which you have rescued. All day long my tongue will talk of your righteous help.

PRAYER—Holy Spirit, powerful Consoler, sacred Bond of the Father and the Son, Hope of the afflicted, descend into my heart and establish in it your loving dominion. Enkindle in my tepid soul the fire of your Love so that I may be wholly subject to you. Amen. **St. Augustine**

FRIDAY
WEEK 5 EASTER SEASON

PSALM 59:9-20 ▪ ZECHARIAH 11 ▪ ACTS 15:22-35 ▪ JOHN 15:12-17

MORNING MEDITATIONS

PRAYER—O eternal Father, in your mercy accept my thanksgiving for bringing me to another day. For this day, and every day of my life, I ask that all my thoughts, words and works will bring glory to you. Heal my infirmities, strengthen my weaknesses, and forgive all my sins, in Jesus' name. Amen. **JW**

PSALM 59:9a, 10a, 16b-17—O my strength, I will watch for you . . . My God in his steadfast love will meet me . . . I will sing aloud your steadfast love in the morning . . . you have been a fortress for me and a refuge in the day of my distress. O my strength, I will sing praises to you, for you, O God, are my fortress, the God who shows me steadfast love.

ZECHARIAH 11:7bc, 10, 14 *Two Kinds of Shepherds*
I became the shepherd of the flock doomed to slaughter. I took two staffs; one I named Favor, the other I named Unity . . . I took my staff Favor and broke it, annulling the covenant that I had made with all the peoples . . . Then I broke my second staff Unity, annulling the family ties between Judah and Israel.

ACTS 15:32, 34b-35 *Encouraging Believers and Proclaiming the Word*
Judas and Silas, who were themselves prophets, said much to encourage and strengthen the believers . . . [Then] they were sent off in peace by the believers to those who had sent them. But Paul and Barnabas remained in Antioch, and there, with many others, they taught and proclaimed the word of the Lord.

JOHN 15:12-17 *Today's Gospel Reading*

> Do not sit trying to manufacture feelings. Ask yourself, "If I were sure that I loved God, what would I do?" When you have found the answer, go and do it.
>
> — C. S. LEWIS, *MERE CHRISTIANITY*

EVENING REFLECTIONS

PSALM 106:4-5—Remember me, O Lord, when you show favor to your people; help me when you deliver them; that I may see the prosperity of your chosen ones, that I may rejoice in the gladness of your nation, that I may glory in your heritage.

PRAYER—Blessed Spirit, when you dwell in us, you also prepare a dwelling for the Father and the Son. Therefore, come to me, Consoler of abandoned souls . . . Help the afflicted, strengthen the weak, and support the wavering. Come and purify me. Amen. **St. Augustine**

SATURDAY
WEEK 5 EASTER SEASON

PSALM 100 ▪ ZECHARIAH 12:1-9 ▪ ACTS 16:1-10 ▪ JOHN 15:18-21

MORNING MEDITATIONS

PRAYER—Savior and Sanctifier of my soul, put your grace in my heart so that I may honor you today with worship in spirit and truth. You have made me and sent me into the world to do your work. Now assist me to fulfill the purpose for which I was born by giving myself gladly to your service. Amen. **JW**

PSALM 100:4-5—Enter his gates with thanksgiving, and his courts with praise. Give thanks to him, bless his name. For the LORD is good; his steadfast love endures forever, and his faithfulness to all generations.

ZECHARIAH 12:5, 8b   *Strength Through the Lord of Hosts*
Then the clans of Judah shall say to themselves, "The inhabitants of Jerusalem have strength through the LORD of hosts, their God.". . . the feeblest among them on that day shall be like David, and the house of David shall be like God, like the angel of the LORD, at their head.

ACTS 16:9-10   *Come Help Us*
During the night Paul had a vision: there stood a man of Macedonia pleading with him and saying, "Come over to Macedonia and help us." When he had seen the vision, we immediately tried to cross over to Macedonia, being convinced that God had called us to proclaim the good news to them.

JOHN 15:18-21   *Today's Gospel Reading*

> The smallest good act today is the capture of a strategic point from which, a few months later, you may be able to go on to victories you never dreamed of.
>
> C. S. LEWIS, *MERE CHRISTIANITY*

EVENING REFLECTIONS

PSALM 75:1, 9—We give thanks to you, O God; we give you thanks; your name is near. People tell of your wondrous deeds . . . I will rejoice forever; I will sing praises to the God of Jacob.

PRAYER—Holy Spirit, powerful Counselor, let no evil desire take possession of me. You love the humble and resist the proud. Come to me, glory of the living, and hope of the dying. Lead me by your grace that I may always be pleasing to you. Amen. **St. Augustine**

WEEK SIX
Easter Season

Ashes to Fire Week 12

Sunday: The Promise of God's Peace

Read the gospel passage from John 14:23-29 and the devotional reflection titled "The Promise of God's Peace," then respond to the discussion prompts in the Reflective Journaling section.

THE MUSIC OF ASHES TO FIRE

Week 12: "Quiet Me" (Track 13)

Monday through Saturday

IN THE MORNING:

A personal daily devotional guide includes prayer, a reading from the Old Testament, the Psalms, the Epistles, and the Gospels for each day of the week.

In addition to the daily psalm, this week's readings come from Zechariah, the Acts of the Apostles, and the gospel of John.

Inspirational quotes from men and women of faith keep us in contact with our shared Christian heritage.

IN THE EVENING:

An evening psalm and prayer become preludes to nighttime rest and renewal.

SUNDAY

Easter Season–Week Six
The Promise of God's Peace

A devotional reflection based on John 14:23-29

*R*ead the gospel passage first, then the devotional reflection that follows. The discussion prompts at the end will help prepare you for Sunday school and small-group sessions.

There are some basic things that virtually every person seems to desire. One of them is peace. We would be hard pressed to find someone who doesn't long for peace. But as much as we want peace, isn't it amazing how elusive peace can be?

No doubt you've experienced this. You get things managed in your life pretty well, the road smooths, and it seems as though things might be peaceful for a while. You breathe out—aah! And just then something unexpected happens, your stomach ties in knots, and your peace shatters. It's hard to hold on to peace. Why is this? If Jesus Christ is the true Source of peace, then why are we not more peace-filled? And if peace is the fruit of the Spirit who indwells us, then why does it seem that peace so often escapes God's people?

Perhaps Jesus gives us an answer in this text. The selected verses have us in the midst of an intense conversation between Jesus and his disciples. Things are coming to a close very quickly in their time together on earth. Jesus is giving them final instructions, trying to help them hold steady through what is about to happen, namely, his passion and death.

He tells them about the Holy Spirit, who will come to fill their hearts with his love and power. The Spirit will teach them everything they need to know. The Spirit will enable them to speak even when they are threatened. The Spirit will support them and comfort them. And the Spirit will give them peace. There it is, the beautiful promise of God's peace spoken with authority by Jesus. "Peace I leave with you; my peace I give you. I do not give to you as the world gives. Do not let your hearts be troubled, and do not let them be afraid" (John 14:27).

We love this verse, and we know it is true. When we have truly opened our hearts to the lordship of Jesus Christ, then we have indeed experienced the "peace of God, which surpasses all understanding" (Phil. 4:7). It's wonderful, but these disciples were experiencing something that we also seem to experience: peace can elude in the face of a threatening world.

It's great to sing "The Peace That Jesus Gives" in church and sense the beautiful assurance of God's presence and help. The challenge comes beyond the safety of the sanctuary, when fear threatens us. The disciples were puzzled about what Jesus was predicting, and soon they would be scared to death at how God was bringing this all to pass.

What these disciples needed to know and what we still need to know is how the promise of peace can last in our hearts. Is there a way that the peace of Christ can truly be the regular experience of our lives? There is a way, but we'll need to be open to hear the answer. The promise of peace spoken by Jesus comes in the midst of a long conversation about obedience. The larger context is Jesus repeatedly saying to his disciples, "If you love me, you will keep my commandments" (John 14:15; see vv. 21, 23). There is a profound connection between peace and obedience.

Perhaps our challenge with living consistently in the peace of Christ is that we desire the peace without the obedience. We want to experience this wonderful rest of spirit, but are we willing to examine truthfully why it eludes us? For example, if we ignore biblical principles of how relationships are to be handled, we probably should not expect to have peace. If we refuse to align our lives with kingdom values, we likely will not know the joy of peace.

If we beg God for peace, but there is unforgiveness in our hearts toward other persons, peace will elude us because we are not following the clear command of Jesus to forgive. If we are pleading with God for peace on Sunday, but Monday through Saturday we are chasing the dreams and values of this world, peace will elude us.

If you want the peace that Jesus gives, live in the truth of Jesus. He said, "Those who love me will keep my word" (v. 23). This is how to know peace. Jesus said, "I do not give to you as the world gives" (v. 27). The peace Jesus gives is no quick-fix peace. It is not a medicated peace. It is not a negotiated peace. It is not peace without price.

Corrie ten Boom, the dear sister who spent years in Hitler's concentration camps, said, "I looked on Jesus and the dove of peace entered my heart. I looked at the dove of peace; and lo . . . off he went."* The peace Jesus gives is a peace that comes to an obedient and loving heart. Do you long for peace? Could you ask yourself these questions?

- Are you seeking first the kingdom of God and his righteousness?
- Are you abiding in Christ daily, spending time with intention in his presence, feeding on his word and being renewed by the Spirit in prayer?
- Are you engaged in acts of service, loving your neighbor as yourself?
- Are your relationships with others characterized by grace, love, and forgiveness?

If you long to know what it is to live in peace, don't just pray that somehow God will drop peace on you. Pray that God will help you to be fully obedient to the model of Jesus. Pray that your heart and life will be "transformed by the renewing of your [mind]" in Christ Jesus (Rom. 12:2). Pray that God will give you grace to make the hard choices of aligning your life to the truth of the gospel.

The peace that Jesus gives comes by grace and in obedience to his commands.
—Jeren Rowell

After reading the passage from John 14:23-29 and the devotional reflection "The Promise of God's Peace," you may also want to read the following related passages:
Acts 16:9-15; Psalm 67; and Revelation 21:10, 22-27; 22:1-5

The discussion prompts that follow will help prepare you to participate in your Sunday school class or small-group study. Use your Reflective Journaling section to record any other insights that come to you as you read the gospel lesson and the devotional reflection.

DISCUSSION PROMPT NO. 1: JOHN 14:23-29
Jesus promises that he and his Father will love and "make our home" (v. 23) with the one who loves him and obeys his teaching. In what ways can we know that we truly love and obey Christ?

DISCUSSION PROMPT NO. 2: JOHN 14:23-29
What does Jesus promise that "the Advocate, the Holy Spirit, whom the Father will send in my name" (v. 26) will do for his followers?

---

*Corrie ten Boom, *Clippings from My Notebook* (Thorndike, ME: Thorndike Press, 1983), 82.

DISCUSSION PROMPT NO. 3: JOHN 14:23-29

In what ways is the peace that Jesus gives different from the peace which "the world gives" (v. 27)?

DISCUSSION PROMPT NO. 4: JOHN 14:23-29

Who do you believe Jesus is referring to when he speaks of "the ruler of this world" (v. 30)? In what ways will even this enemy confirm the truth of Jesus' life and ministry?

DISCUSSION PROMPT NO. 5: DEVOTIONAL REFLECTION

We are challenged to "Pray that God will give [us] grace to make the hard choices of aligning [our lives] to the truth of the gospel." What are some areas of your life that need to be brought into alignment with God's will? What are some steps you can take today so that you can live in Christ's peace?

Reflective Journaling

MONDAY | WEEK 6 EASTER SEASON

PSALM 149:1-9 ▪ **ZECHARIAH 12:10—13:1** ▪ **ACTS 16:11-15** ▪ **JOHN 15:26—16:4**

MORNING MEDITATION

PRAYER—O God, you are the giver of all good gifts and I desire to praise your name for all of your goodness to me. I thank you for sending your Son to die for my sins, for the means of grace, and for the hope of glory, through Jesus Christ. Amen. **JW**

PSALM 149:2, 4—Let Israel be glad in its Maker; let the children of Zion rejoice in their King . . . For the LORD takes pleasure in his people; he adorns the humble with victory.

ZECHARIAH 12:10; 13:1 *A Fountain Shall Be Opened*
And I will pour out a spirit of compassion and supplication on the house of David and the inhabitants of Jerusalem, so that, when they look on the one whom they have pierced, they shall mourn for him . . . On that day a fountain shall be opened for the house of David and the inhabitants of Jerusalem, to cleanse them from sin and iniquity.

ACTS 16:14-15b *She Listened Eagerly*
A certain woman named Lydia, a worshiper of God, was listening to us . . . the Lord opened her heart to listen eagerly to what was said by Paul. When she and her household were baptized, she urged us, saying, ". . . Come and stay at my home."

JOHN 15:26—16:4 *The Gospel Reading*

> The Gospel offers a person life. Never offer people a thimbleful of Gospel. Do not offer them merely joy, or merely peace, or merely rest, or merely safety; tell them how Christ came to give us a more abundant life, a life abundant in love.
>
> HENRY DRUMMOND, *THE GREATEST THING IN THE WORLD*

EVENING REFLECTIONS

PSALM 79:8-9—Do not remember against us the iniquities of our ancestors; let your compassion come speedily to meet us . . . Help us, O God of our salvation, for the glory of your name; deliver us, and forgive our sins, for your name's sake.

PRAYER—O God, I give you my affections: my love, my fear, my joy. What you love may I love. What displeases you, may it displease me. I give you my body. May I glorify you with it, and preserve it holy, fit for you to dwell in. May I neither indulge it, nor abuse it, but keep it healthy, vigorous, and active and fit to serve you with all my heart. Amen. **JW**

TUESDAY
WEEK 6
EASTER SEASON

PSALM 138:1-3, 7-8 ▪ **ZECHARIAH 13:2-6** ▪ **ACTS 16:22-34** ▪ **JOHN 16:5-11**

MORNING MEDITATION

PRAYER—O God, put your grace into my heart so I may praise your great and glorious name. You have made me, and you send me into the world to do your work. Assist me to fulfill the purpose of my creation, and to show my praise by giving myself to your service. Amen. **JW**

PSALM 138:2-3—I bow down toward your holy temple and give thanks to your name for your steadfast love and your faithfulness; for you have exalted your name and your word above everything. On the day I called, you answered me, you increased my strength of soul.

ZECHARIAH 13:6 *What Are These Wounds?*
And if anyone asks them, "What are these wounds on your chest?" the answer will be "The wounds I received in the house of my friends."

ACTS 16:29-31 *Believe on the Lord Jesus*
The jailor . . . fell down trembling before Paul and Silas . . . and said, "Sirs, what must I do to be saved?" They answered, "Believe on the Lord Jesus, and you will be saved, you and your household."

JOHN 16:5-11 *The Gospel Reading*

> To love abundantly is to live abundantly, and to love forever is to live forever. Hence, eternal life is inextricably bound up with love . . . Eternal life is also to know God, and God is love. This is Christ's own definition. Ponder it. "This is life eternal, that they might know you the only true God and Jesus Christ whom you have sent." Love must be eternal. It is what God is. — HENRY DRUMMOND, *THE GREATEST THING IN THE WORLD*

EVENING REFLECTIONS

PSALM 78:4, 7—We will tell to the coming generation the glorious deeds of the LORD, and his might, and the wonders that he has done . . . so that they should set their hope in God, and not forget the works of God, but keep his commandments.

PRAYER—O God, your Son was despised and rejected. When I am slighted by my friends, or disdained by my superiors, or ridiculed by my equals, then I will simply pray, "It is now that I begin to be a disciple of Christ." Amen. **JW**

WEDNESDAY
WEEK 6 EASTER SEASON

PSALM 148:1-2, 11-14 ▪ **ZECHARIAH 13:7-9** ▪ **ACTS 17:15, 22—18:1** ▪ **JOHN 16:12-15**

MORNING MEDITATION

PRAYER—Lord God . . . accept my thanks for keeping me through the night, and may I be wholly devoted to your service today. Send your Holy Spirit to be my guide, the sanctifier of my soul and body. Save, defend and build me up in your fear and love. Amen. *JW*

PSALM 148:1, 11a, 13—Praise the Lord! Praise the Lord from the heavens; praise him in the heights . . . [Let] kings of the earth and all peoples . . . praise the name of the Lord, for his name alone is exalted; his glory is above earth and heaven.

ZECHARIAH 13:9bc *I Will Answer*
They will call on my name, and I will answer them. I will say, "They are my people"; and they will say, "The Lord is our God."

ACTS 17:24a, 26-28a *He Is Not Far from Us*
The God who made the world and everything in it . . . made all nations to inhabit the whole earth, and he allotted the times of their existence and the boundaries of the places where they would live, so that they would search for God and perhaps grope for him and find him—though indeed he is not far from each one of us. For "In him we live and move and have our being."

JOHN 16:12-15 *The Gospel Reading*

> "We love—because He first loved us." Look at the word "because" . . . The effect follows that we love . . . We cannot help it. Because he loved us, we love, we love everybody . . . Contemplate the love of Christ and you will love.
>
> HENRY DRUMMOND, *THE GREATEST THING IN THE WORLD*

EVENING REFLECTIONS

PSALM 8:3-4a, 5—When I look at your heavens, the work of your fingers . . . what are human beings that you are mindful of them . . . You have made them a little lower than God, and crowned them with glory and honor.

PRAYER—O God the Father, have mercy on me. O God the Son, who knowing the will of the Father, came into the world to save me, have mercy on me. O God the Holy Spirit who has breathed holy thoughts in me, have mercy on me. Holy Trinity, I adore you as One God. Have mercy on me. Amen. *JW*

THURSDAY
WEEK 6 — EASTER SEASON

PSALM 47:1-8 ▪ ZECHARIAH 14:1-8 ▪ ACTS 18:1-9 ▪ JOHN 16:16-20

MORNING MEDITATION

PRAYER—Lord Jesus, help me with your grace so that whatever I do and experience today it may bring glory to you. Increase my love for you and for all people. Direct my paths and teach me to keep you always before me. Amen. **JW**

PSALM 47:1-2, 5a, 6b, 8—Clap your hands, all you peoples; shout to God with songs of joy. For the LORD, the Most High, is awesome, a great king over all the earth . . . God has gone up with a shout . . . sing praises to our King, sing praises . . . God is king over the nations; God sits on his holy throne.

ZECHARIAH 14:4a, 4c, 5c, 8a *Living Waters Shall Flow*
On that day his feet shall stand on the Mount of Olives . . . and [it] shall be split in two from east to west by a very wide valley . . . Then the LORD my God will come, and all the holy ones with him . . . On that day living waters shall flow out from Jerusalem.

ACTS 18:1, 5 *Jesus Is the Messiah*
After this Paul left Athens and went to Corinth . . . When Silas and Timothy arrived from Macedonia, Paul was occupied with proclaiming the word, testifying to the Jews that the Messiah was Jesus.

JOHN 16:16-20 *The Gospel Reading*

> Look at this Perfect Character, this Perfect Life. Look at the great Sacrifice as he laid down himself, all through life, and upon the cross, and you must love him. And loving him, you must become like him. Love begets love. HENRY DRUMMOND, *THE GREATEST THING IN THE WORLD*

EVENING REFLECTIONS

PSALM 24:3-5—Who can ascend the hill of the LORD? And who shall stand in his holy place? Those who have clean hands and pure hearts, who do not lift up their souls to what is false, and do not swear deceitfully. They will receive blessing from the LORD, and vindication from the God of their salvation.

PRAYER—O God my Savior and Sanctifier, give me the mind that is in you. Let me learn to be meek and lowly, and pour into me the whole spirit of divine humility. Fill every part of my soul with it, and make it the ruling habit of both mind and heart. Amen. **JW**

FRIDAY
WEEK 6
EASTER SEASON

PSALM 96:1-4, 8-9 ▪ ZECHARIAH 14:9-15 ▪ ACTS 18:9-18 ▪ JOHN 16:20-23

MORNING MEDITATIONS

PRAYER—Father in heaven, let me see your glory, even if it must be from the shelter of the cleft of the rock and from beneath the protection of your covering hand. Whatever the cost to me in loss of friends or goods or length of days, let me know you as you are, that I may adore you as I should. Amen.

PSALM 96:1a, 8-9—Sing to the Lord a new song . . . Ascribe to the Lord the glory due his name; bring an offering, and come into his courts. Worship the Lord in holy splendor; tremble before him all the earth.

ZECHARIAH 14:9, 10b, 11 *The Lord Will Become King*
The Lord will become king over all the earth; on that day the Lord will be one and his name one . . . Jerusalem shall remain aloft on its site . . . And it shall be inhabited, for never again shall it be doomed to destruction; Jerusalem shall abide in security.

ACTS 18:9-10 *I Am with You*
One night the Lord said to Paul in a vision, "Do not be afraid, but speak and do not be silent; for I am with you, and no one will lay a hand on you to harm you, for there are many in this city who are my people."

JOHN 16:20-23 *Today's Gospel Reading*

> Where Love is, God is. He that dwells in Love dwells in God. God is Love. Therefore, *love*. Without distinction, without calculation, without procrastination, love.
>
> HENRY DRUMMOND, *THE GREATEST THING IN THE WORLD*

EVENING REFLECTIONS

PSALM 85:7-8—Show us your steadfast love, O Lord, and grant us your salvation. Let me hear what God the Lord will speak, for he will speak peace to his people, . . . to those who turn to him in their hearts.

PRAYER—My Lord and my God, I know that unless I am planted together with you in the likeness of your death that I cannot share in your resurrection. Strengthen me, that by denying myself and taking up my cross daily, I may crucify all that is not like you, and utterly destroy all sin. Amen. **JW**

SATURDAY
WEEK 6 — EASTER SEASON

PSALM 47:2-3, 8-9 ▪ ZECHARIAH 14:16-21 ▪ ACTS 18:23-28 ▪ JOHN 16:23b-28

MORNING MEDITATIONS

PRAYER—O God, I give you my understanding. May it be my first concern to know you, your perfection, your works and your will. Silence any reasonings that conflict with what you teach me. I give you my will; may it always submit to yours. May I will your glory in all things; delighting to do your will and rejoicing in it. Amen. *JW*

PSALM 47:8-9—God is king over the nations; God sits upon his holy throne. The princes of the peoples gather as the people of the God of Abraham. For the shields of the earth belong to God; he is highly exalted.

ZECHARIAH 14:20-21a *Holy to the Lord*
On that day there shall be inscribed on the bells of the horses, "Holy to the Lord." And the cooking pots in the house of the Lord shall be as holy as the bowls in front of the altar; and every cooking pot in Jerusalem and Judah shall be sacred to the Lord of hosts.

ACTS 18:25, 28 *Accurate Teaching*
[Apollos] had been instructed in the Way of the Lord; and he spoke with burning enthusiasm and taught accurately the things concerning Jesus . . . for he powerfully refuted the Jews in public, showing by the scriptures that the Messiah is Jesus.

JOHN 16:23b-28 *Today's Gospel Reading*

> The supreme work to which we need to address ourselves in this world is to learn Love. Is life not full of opportunities for learning love? . . . Love is not a thing of enthusiastic emotion. It is a rich and vigorous expression of the whole of Christian character—the Christlike nature in its fullest development.
>
> HENRY DRUMMOND, *THE GREATEST THING IN THE WORLD*

EVENING REFLECTIONS

PSALM 90:12, 17—Teach us to count our days that we may gain a wise heart . . . Let the favor of the Lord our God be upon us, and prosper for us the work of our hands—O prosper the work of our hands!

PRAYER—O Father of mercy, accept my humble thanks for your watchful care today. Continue to show me your loving-kindness, and protect me through the night. Let your holy angels watch over me and defend me. Let me rest in peace and rise with eagerness to serve you. Amen. *JW*

WEEK SEVEN
Easter Season

Ashes to Fire Week 13

Sunday: As Long As It Takes

Read the gospel passage from John 17:20-26 and the devotional reflection titled "As Long As It Takes," then respond to the discussion prompts in the Reflective Journaling section.

THE MUSIC OF ASHES TO FIRE

Week 13: "Lo, He Comes With Clouds Descending" (Track 14)

Monday through Saturday

IN THE MORNING:

A personal daily devotional guide includes prayer, a reading from the Old Testament, the Psalms, the Epistles, and the Gospels for each day of the week.

In addition to the daily psalm, this week's readings come from Malachi, the Acts of the Apostles, and the gospel of John.

Inspirational quotes from men and women of faith keep us in contact with our shared Christian heritage.

IN THE EVENING:

An evening psalm and prayer become preludes to nighttime rest and renewal.

ASCENSION SUNDAY

Easter Season–Week Seven
As Long As It Takes

**A devotional reflection based on John 17:20-26
(and other gospel sources)**

Read the gospel passage first, then the devotional reflection that follows. The discussion prompts at the end will help prepare you for Sunday school and small-group sessions.

(Two disciples conversing in the upper room one week before Pentecost)

DISCIPLE ONE: Three days now since Jesus left us . . .

DISCIPLE TWO: I know. I still can hardly believe what we saw. I thought I'd be sad to see him go, but instead I've never felt so—so alive! I'm feeling renewed! I know something joyful is about to happen!

DISCIPLE ONE: Yes, I felt it then too. Jesus looked right at me when he was blessing us. But then remember what we saw? He rose up, up above the palms, and then a cloud suddenly was there. It was almost as if he stepped through a curtain, and he was gone!

DISCIPLE TWO: He said we were to wait, not to leave town. Everybody is here. I wonder just what it is we are waiting for? Three days already!

DISCIPLE ONE: Could we be waiting for what he called the promise of the Father? He did reassure us that it wouldn't be many days until we would be "baptized with the Holy Spirit." Those were his words!

DISCIPLE TWO: I wonder what that could possibly mean.

DISCIPLE ONE: This upper room where we're meeting—it brings back such powerful memories. He sat right over *there* that night he served as our Passover host!

DISCIPLE TWO: He washed our feet—right here! Remember how Peter got so upset. I was too embarrassed to speak.

DISCIPLE ONE: I remember. I was more awestruck when he broke the bread and said, "This is my body," and then passed the cup and said, "This is my blood." We were all silent then.

DISCIPLE TWO: I'll never forget it. It's hard to grasp all that has happened since that night. But even after all that, what I can't get out of my mind is *that prayer*.

DISCIPLE ONE: Hmm! How could I forget? He prayed so fervently for you and me—for all of us!

DISCIPLE TWO: You know, somehow it all fits together—the reason we're back here in this upper room. That prayer Jesus prayed here. Then all that has happened since—and now our waiting.

DISCIPLE ONE: What do you mean? "Fits together"?

DISCIPLE TWO: The blood! The broken bread! Passover! *That's* what the Baptist meant when he said Jesus is the "Lamb of God"! I know somehow our sins went with Jesus to the cross. But then there's the resurrection, and ever since, Jesus has been getting us ready for something new.

DISCIPLE ONE: So why did Jesus have to go away now that the battle is over? Why not set up his throne in Jerusalem right now?

DISCIPLE TWO: He didn't say the battle is over. Remember what he did say? "All authority in heaven and on earth has been given to me" [Matt. 28:18]. And then he told us to come here and wait, and then he went away.

DISCIPLE ONE: Didn't he promise he would never leave us? So why has he gone away and left us? What is that?

DISCIPLE TWO: Maybe he didn't leave us at all! Maybe he is a lot closer than you know.

DISCIPLE ONE: But he did! He did leave us! Didn't he?

DISCIPLE TWO: Think about this: You know how the high priest in the temple makes atonement on the High Holy Day? How he goes behind the curtain, out of sight? I knew right then as Jesus went into that cloud where he was going. He said he was going to his Father—and our Father [see John 20:17]!

DISCIPLE ONE: What do the high priest and the temple have to do with it?

DISCIPLE TWO: Don't you see? It's not into the holy place in the temple but into the actual presence of God where Jesus went. Jesus is the true high priest of God! I'm not the only one who had that thought, and I believe that Jesus wants us to wait so we can know for certain.

DISCIPLE ONE: Those two men did say he was coming back . . .

DISCIPLE TWO: The high priest always comes back. He gives the assurance that the sacrifice is accepted. Maybe that's why we're waiting.

DISCIPLE ONE: Oh, I think I see what you're saying.

DISCIPLE TWO: His praying was so fervent—affecting all of us as he kept talking, praying, about how we are loved by the Father just as the Father loves him [17:23]. Remember how he asked the Father in heaven to make us one, one with himself and one with each other [vv. 21, 23]? Maybe as we're waiting, we can be praying about our unity.

DISCIPLE ONE: There are so many of us here. How can we ever "be one"?

DISCIPLE TWO: I don't know, but we're working on it. Every morning, all day—eating, praying, and remembering together.

DISCIPLE ONE: How long do you think it will be before he comes back? What is that promise he was talking about?

DISCIPLE TWO: I don't have any idea. As long as it takes—we'll do exactly what Jesus asked us to do. He never once misled us. As long as it takes, we'll wait.

DISCIPLE ONE: Did you notice that people have started arriving for the Pentecost feast this next weekend?

DISCIPLE TWO: Jews from all over the world will be here. The inns will be packed. The streets will be full. I'm glad we at least have this big room to use while we're waiting.

DISCIPLE ONE: As long as it takes! —Russell F. Metcalfe Jr.

After reading the passage from John 17:20-26 and the devotional reflection "As Long As It Takes," you may also want to read the following related passages:

Acts 16:16-34; Psalm 97; Revelation 22:12-14, 16-17, 20-21

The discussion prompts that follow will help prepare you to participate in your Sunday school class or small-group study. Use your Reflective Journaling section to record any other insights that come to you as you read the gospel lesson and the devotional reflection.

DISCUSSION PROMPT NO. 1: JOHN 17:20-26

What specific requests does Jesus make of the Father for those who will believe in him through the disciples' teaching?

DISCUSSION PROMPT NO. 2: JOHN 17:20-26

What do you believe Jesus meant by "completely one" (v. 23) among his followers?

DISCUSSION PROMPT NO. 3: JOHN 17:20-26

In what ways will the unity Jesus describes become a witness to the truth of his life and the Father's love for his followers?

DISCUSSION PROMPT NO. 4: JOHN 17:20-26

What does Jesus long to see happen in the lives of all who follow him?

DISCUSSION PROMPT NO. 5: DEVOTIONAL REFLECTION

What is the significance of the high priest's returning from the temple's holy place? In what ways can we continue to fulfill Jesus' prayer for his disciples?

Reflective Journaling

MONDAY | WEEK 7 EASTER SEASON

PSALM 68:1-10 • MALACHI 1:6-11; 2:4-7 • ACTS 19:1-8 • JOHN 16:29-33

MORNING MEDITATIONS

PRAYER—O God, you are the giver of all good gifts and I desire to praise your name for all of your goodness to me. I thank you for sending your Son to die for my sins, for the means of grace, and for the hope of glory, through Jesus Christ. Amen. *JW*

PSALM 68:1, 3-4—Let God rise up, let his enemies be scattered . . . Let the righteous be joyful; let them exult before God; let them be jubilant with joy. Sing to God, sing praises to his name . . . his name is the Lord—be exultant before him!

MALACHI 1:11 *My Name Is Great*
For from the rising of the sun to its setting my name is great among the nations, and in every place incense is offered to my name, and a pure offering; for my name is great among the nations, says the Lord of hosts.

ACTS 19:2, 6a *The Holy Spirit Came upon Them*
[Paul] said to them, "Did you receive the Holy Spirit when you became believers?" They replied, "No, we have not even heard that there is a Holy Spirit" . . . When Paul had laid his hands on them, the Holy Spirit came upon them.

JOHN 16:29-33 *Today's Gospel Reading*

> Only the Spirit of the Holy One can impart to the human spirit the knowledge of the holy. Yet as electric power flows only through a conductor, so the Spirit flows through truth and must find some measure of truth in the mind before he can illuminate the heart.
>
> A. W. TOZER, *THE KNOWLEDGE OF THE HOLY*

EVENING REFLECTIONS

PSALM 89:15-16, 18—Happy are the people who know the festal shout, who walk, O Lord, in the light of your countenance; they exult in your name all day long, and extol your righteousness . . . For our shield belongs to the Lord, our king to the Holy One of Israel.

PRAYER—My Lord and my God, you see my heart; and my desires are not hidden from you. I am encouraged and strengthened by your goodness to me today. I want to be yours and yours alone, O God, my Savior, my Sanctifier. Hear me, help me, show mercy to me for Jesus Christ's sake. Amen. *JW*

TUESDAY
WEEK 7 · EASTER SEASON

PSALM 68:11-20 ▪ MALACHI 3:1-4 ▪ ACTS 20:17-24 ▪ JOHN 17:1-11a

MORNING MEDITATIONS

PRAYER—O God, let your unwearied and tender love to me make my love unwearied and tender toward my neighbors, always fervent in my prayers for their health, safety, ease, and happiness. Make me peaceful, easy to forgive, and glad to return good for evil. Amen. **JW**

PSALM 68:19-20—Blessed be the Lord, who daily bears us up; God is our salvation, who bears our burdens. Our God is a God of salvation, and to GOD, the Lord, belongs escape from death.

MALACHI 3:2b-3 *A Refiner's Fire*
For he is like a refiner's fire and like fullers' soap; he will sit as a refiner and purifier of silver, and he will purify the descendants of Levi and refine them like gold and silver, until they present offerings to the LORD in righteousness.

ACTS 20:24 *I Testify to the Good News*
But I do not count my life of any value to myself, if I only may finish my course and the ministry that I received from the Lord Jesus, to testify to the good news of God's grace.

JOHN 17:1-11a *Today's Gospel Reading*

> Holy is the way God is. To be holy he does not conform to a standard. He is that standard. He is absolutely holy with an infinite, incomprehensible fullness of purity that is incapable of being other than it is. Because he is holy, his attributes are holy; that is, whatever we think of as belonging to God must be thought of as holy.
>
> A. W. TOZER, *THE KNOWLEDGE OF THE HOLY*

EVENING REFLECTIONS

PSALM 95:1, 6-7—Come, let us sing to the LORD . . . Come, let us worship and bow down, let us kneel before the LORD, our Maker. For he is our God, and we are the people of his pasture, and the sheep of his hand.

PRAYER—Father, help me to remember you as I fall asleep, and as well think upon you when I first awaken. You have preserved me from all the dangers of the past day, you support me in trials, and hide me under the shadow of your wings. So let me sleep through this night in your comfort and peace. Amen. **JW**

WEDNESDAY
WEEK 7 EASTER SEASON

PSALM 68:1-4, 32-36 ▪ MALACHI 3:5-7 ▪ ACTS 20:25-38 ▪ JOHN 17:11b-19

MORNING MEDITATIONS

PRAYER—Lord God, send your Holy Spirit to be the guide of all my ways, and the sanctifier of my soul and body. Give me the light of your presence, your peace from heaven, and the salvation of my soul, through Jesus Christ my Lord. Amen. *JW*

PSALM 68:32, 35—Sing to God, O kingdoms of the earth; sing praises to the Lord . . . Awesome is God in his sanctuary, the God of Israel; he gives power and strength to his people! Blessed be God!

MALACHI 3:6, 7b   *I Do Not Change*
For I the LORD do not change; therefore you, O children of Jacob, have not perished . . . Return to me, and I will return to you, says the LORD of hosts.

ACTS 20:27-28   *I Do Not Shrink*
I did not shrink from declaring to you the whole purpose of God. Keep watch over yourselves and over all the flock, of which the Holy Spirit has made you overseers, to shepherd the church of God that he obtained with the blood of his own Son.

JOHN 17:11b-19   *Today's Gospel Reading*

> The apostles themselves, though on many occasions they had been strengthened by our Lord's miracles and instructed by his words, still panicked at the atrocities of his passion, and only after some hesitation accepted the truth of his resurrection. But his ascension wrought such a change in them that whatever before had been a source of fear now became a source of great joy for them.   ST. LEO THE GREAT, *SERMON 2 ON THE ASCENSION*

EVENING REFLECTIONS

PSALM 119:129-130, 135—Your decrees are wonderful; therefore my soul keeps them. The unfolding of your words gives light; it imparts understanding to the simple . . . Make your face shine upon your servant, and teach me your statutes.

PRAYER—Hear my prayers, O most merciful Father, through the mediation of Jesus Christ our Redeemer, who with you and the Holy Spirit is worshipped and glorified among the saints, one God, blessed forever. Amen. *JW*

THURSDAY
WEEK 7 — EASTER SEASON

PSALM 16:1-2, 5-11 ▪ MALACHI 3:8-15 ▪ ACTS 22:30—23:11 ▪ JOHN 17:20-26

MORNING MEDITATIONS

PRAYER—Father, I give you myself and my all; let me look upon myself to have nothing outside of you. Be the sole ruler of life, and when I am tempted to prefer conformity to the world, or the company and customs of those around me, may my answer be, "I am not my own." I am not for myself, nor for the world, but for God alone. God be merciful to your servant. Amen. *JW*

PSALM 16:9-11—Therefore my heart is glad, and my soul rejoices; my body also rests secure. For you do not give me up to Sheol, or let your faithful one see the Pit. You show me the path of life. In your presence there is fullness of joy; in your right hand are pleasures forevermore.

MALACHI 3:10   *An Overflowing Blessing*
Bring the full tithe into the storehouse, so that there may be food in my house, and thus put me to the test, says the LORD of hosts; see if I will not open the windows of heaven for you and pour down for you an overflowing blessing.

ACTS 23:11   *Keep Up Your Courage*
That night the Lord stood near him and said, "Keep up your courage! For just as you have testified for me in Jerusalem, so you must bear witness also in Rome."

JOHN 17:20-26   *Today's Gospel Reading*

> Because humanity needed to be cured of its ancient wounds and cleansed of the filth of sin, the only begotten Son of God became the son of man, too, lacking nothing of the reality of manhood and nothing of the fullness of deity.
>
> ST. LEO THE GREAT, *SERMON 15 ON THE PASSION*

EVENING REFLECTIONS

PSALM 105:1, 3-4—Give thanks to the LORD, call on his name, make known his deeds among the peoples . . . Glory in his holy name; let the hearts of those who seek the LORD rejoice. Seek the Lord and his strength; seek his presence continually.

PRAYER—Eternal God, my Sovereign Lord, I acknowledge all I am, all I have is yours. I humbly thank you for all the blessings you have bestowed upon me—for creating me in your own image, for redeeming me by the death of your blessed Son, and for the assistance of the Holy Spirit, through Christ I pray. Amen. *JW*

FRIDAY | WEEK 7 EASTER SEASON

PSALM 103:1-2, 11-13, 19-20 • MALACHI 3:16-18 • ACTS 26:19-32 • JOHN 21:15-19

MORNING MEDITATIONS

PRAYER—Father of my Lord, watch over me today with eyes of mercy, direct my soul and body according to your will, and fill my heart with your Holy Spirit, that I may live this day, and all the rest of my days, to your glory. Amen. *JW*

PSALM 103:11-13—For as the heavens are high above the earth, so great is his steadfast love toward those who fear him; as far as the east is from the west, so far he removes our transgressions from us. As a father has compassion for his children, so the LORD has compassion for those who fear him.

MALACHI 3:17 *My Special Possession*
They shall be mine, says the LORD of hosts, my special possession on the day when I act, and I will spare them as parents spare their children who serve them.

ACTS 26:19b-20 *I Was Not Disobedient to the Heavenly Vision*
I was not disobedient to the heavenly vision, but declared . . . that [all] should repent and turn to God and do deeds consistent with repentance.

JOHN 21:15-19 *Today's Gospel Reading*

> For in the darkness and ignorance of this life, [the Holy Spirit] is the light which enlightens the lowly of spirit; he is the love which draws us; he is the sweetening presence; he our approach to God; he the love of the loving; he is devotion; he is piety.
>
> WILLIAM OF SAINT-THIERRY, *MIRROR OF CHARITY*

EVENING REFLECTIONS

PSALM 102:12-13, 16—You, O LORD, are enthroned forever; your name endures to all generations. You will rise up and have compassion on Zion, for it is time to favor it; the appointed time has come . . . For the LORD will build up Zion; he will appear in his glory.

PRAYER—Almighty God, I bless you from my heart. O Savior of the World, God of God, Light of Light you have destroyed the power of the devil, you have overcome death, and you sit at the right hand of the Father. Be to me light and peace and make me a new creature, through Christ my Lord. Amen. *JW*

SATURDAY
WEEK 7 — EASTER SEASON

PSALM 11 ▪ MALACHI 4 ▪ ACTS 28:16-20, 30-31 ▪ JOHN 21:20-25

MORNING MEDITATIONS

PRAYER—Glory to you, O Blessed Spirit, who comes to us from the Father and the Son. You came down in tongues of fire on the apostles on the first day of the week, enabling them to preach the good news of salvation to a sinful world. Now move in my heart and among your people, as you once moved over the face of the great deep. Bring us all out of that dark chaos into newness of resurrection life, through Christ our Lord. Amen. *JW*

PSALM 11:4, 7—The LORD is in his holy temple; the LORD's throne is in heaven. His eyes behold, his gaze examines humankind . . . For the LORD is righteous; he loves righteous deeds; the upright shall behold his face.

MALACHI 4:2, 5   *The Sun of Righteousness Shall Rise*
For you who revere my name the sun of righteousness shall rise, with healing in its wings. You shall go out leaping like calves from the stall . . . Lo, I will send you the prophet Elijah before the great and terrible day of the LORD comes.

ACTS 28:30-31   *He Proclaimed Christ*
[Paul] lived there two whole years . . . and welcomed all who came to him, proclaiming the kingdom of God and teaching about the Lord Jesus Christ with all boldness and without hindrance.

JOHN 21:20-25   *Today's Gospel Reading*

> So then, make yourselves worthy so that Christ will be in your midst. For where peace is, there Christ is because Christ is Peace. And where righteousness is, Christ is there because Christ is Righteousness. Let Him be in the midst of you, so that you can see Him.
>
> ST. AMBROSE, *EPISTLE 63*

EVENING REFLECTIONS

PSALM 33:1, 21-22—Rejoice in the LORD, O you righteous. Praise befits the upright . . . Our heart is glad in him, because we trust in his holy name. Let your steadfast love, O LORD, be upon us, even as we hope in you.

PRAYER—Now to God the Father who first loved us, and made us accepted in the Beloved; to God the Son who loved us and washed us from our sins in his own blood; to God the Holy Spirit who spreads the love of God abroad in our hearts, be all love and all glory for time and eternity. Amen! *JW*

Pentecost Sunday

Ashes to Fire Week 14

Sunday: Pentecost: The Fullness of Life in the Spirit

Read the gospel passages from John 14:8-17, 25-27 and the selection from Acts 2:1-21, and then read the devotional reflection titled "The Fullness of Life in the Spirit." Respond to the discussion prompts in the Reflective Journaling section.

THE MUSIC OF ASHES TO FIRE

Week 14: "O Breath of Life" (Track 15)

O Breath of Life

O Breath of Life, come sweeping through us;
Revive Thy Church with life and pow'r.
O Breath of Life, come, cleanse, renew us;
And fit Thy Church to meet this hour.
O Heart of Christ, once broken for us,
'Tis there we find our strength and rest;
Our broken, contrite hearts now solace,
And let Thy waiting Church be blest.
O Breath of Love, come breathe within us,
Renewing thought and will and heart.
Come, love of Christ, afresh to win us;
Revive Thy Church in ev'ry part.

—Bessie Porter Head

PENTECOST SUNDAY

PENTECOST
The Fullness of Life in the Spirit

A devotional reflection based on John 14:8-17, 25-27

Read the gospel passage first, then the devotional reflection that follows. The discussion prompts at the end will help prepare you for Sunday school and small-group sessions.

I just hate doing it—saying good-bye to a close friend at the airport. I did it again this week. We talked rapidly for the last hour about everything we could think to say to each other as we walked slowly to the security door where we parted ways. We hoped to slow the clock by not looking at it. Who knows when we'll see each other again? I know we can phone and email each other from across the country, but it's just not the same as being together. Saying good-bye and walking away from a close friend is so hard!

That's exactly how Jesus and the disciples felt in our text as they talked together that night following the Last Supper. Jesus wanted to leave his followers with important parting words, and he'd saved the best for last. He closed their time together by giving them the powerful promise of the coming Holy Spirit. His disciples had no idea who he was talking about; they failed to grasp the concept.

Jesus knew as he left his disciples that they would need more than a motivational speech to carry on the ministry he had started in our world. They had the Jewish religious establishment and the Roman government working against them, not to mention their own group's personal relationship struggles and their individual, internal fears. Jesus knew they would be defeated before he returned to the Father and his work on earth could be lost. They needed Someone to come alongside them to act as a Counselor, Comforter, Helper, and Enabler.

So Jesus spent those precious last moments together talking to his disciples about the coming of the Holy Spirit and the need for them to prepare their hearts for his arrival. In John 14:15 Jesus emphasized a central difference between the Old and New Testaments. In the Old Testament people tended to concentrate on following rules, which quickly led to checklists that could be physically or mentally reviewed daily to judge godly performance. The New Testament shifted the center of attention to living in a loving relationship with God. We follow the commandments because we love Jesus, not because the checklist says we have to perform certain deeds. But even the motivation of love falls short of accomplishing our goal every time. We need the assistance of the Holy Spirit both to live in relationship with God and to do his will each day.

Jesus obviously could not tell his disciples everything he wanted them to know. They had much more to learn in the days, months, and years to come. The Holy Spirit would carry on his teaching ministry in their lives as he led them "into all the truth" (16:13). Jesus knew that by directing his disciples to wait for the Holy Spirit's coming he was pointing them in the direction of the truth they would need to carry on his work and get the fledgling Christian church started on the right foot.

Perhaps the most cryptic promise Jesus made that night to his disciples came at the end of John 14:17: "You know him [the Spirit of truth], because he abides with you, and he will be in you." Two little words in the English language make a world of difference in daily life: "with" and "in." At first glance, we think of this new Friend Jesus promised being *with* his disciples to assist them as Counselor, Comforter, Helper, and Enabler. Now Jesus shifted the promise to the revolutionary notion of this new Friend being *in* them. The disciples could not possibly have fully grasped what Jesus tried to communicate that evening. No doubt they pondered those final words over and over in their minds as they waited in the upper room following his crucifixion, resurrection, and return to His Father.

Jesus closed his promise of the coming Holy Spirit by leaving his disciples his legacy. Before a person leaves this earth we often recount his or her final conversations and what subjects drew his or her attention. Jesus' attention was centered on leaving his disciples his peace (vv. 26-27). People often want to validate their religious experience with unusual events, signs, or wonders. They hunger for an astonishing experience or a breathtaking feeling. Jesus said in John 14 that following him meant loving him, living in relationship with his Father through the Holy Spirit, and sensing his peace. A deep sense of peace—that's the priceless result of the Holy Spirit's presence abiding within our hearts.

Jesus' promise to his disciples of the Holy Spirit's coming became a blessed reality on the Day of Pentecost. Immediately his disciples experienced the Holy Spirit's residence within their hearts in a way undeniable, a way unexplainable, and a way they would never get over! The Day of Pentecost revolutionized everything about their walk with God. What's more, they made a wonderful discovery. They recognized the presence of the Holy Spirit in their hearts as none other than a different manifestation of the same God they had known when they walked and talked with Jesus Christ. Suddenly, those words from John 14:18 made sense, "I will not leave you orphaned; I am coming to you." The Holy Spirit brought them the presence of the living Christ.

Now because of Pentecost, those first disciples—and all who follow after them—can live the fullness of life in the Spirit of Christ! Live in his fullness today and every day. —Frank Moore

After reading the passage from John 14:8-17, 25-27 and the devotional reflection "The Fullness of Life in the Spirit," you may also want to read the following related passages:

Acts 2:1-21; Psalm 104:24-34, 35b; Romans 8:14-17

The discussion prompts that follow will help prepare you to participate in your Sunday school class or small-group study. Use your Reflective Journaling section to record any other insights that come to you as you read the gospel lesson and the devotional reflection.

DISCUSSION PROMPT NO. 1: JOHN 14:8-17, 25-27

In what ways does Jesus in his life, teachings, death, and resurrection "show us the Father" (v. 9)?

DISCUSSION PROMPT NO. 2: JOHN 14:8-17, 25-27

How do you understand what Jesus means when he says that the one who believes in him "will do greater works than these" (v. 12)?

DISCUSSION PROMPT NO. 3: JOHN 14:8-17, 25-27

How would you explain the difference between the Advocate, the Holy Spirit, being "with" Jesus' disciples and later "in" them (vv. 16-17)?

DISCUSSION PROMPT NO. 4: JOHN 14:8-17, 25-27

What are the specific promises Jesus makes to his faithful followers in this passage? How does it make you feel that these promises are yours?

DISCUSSION PROMPT NO. 5: DEVOTIONAL REFLECTION

Have you experienced Jesus' promise of the abiding presence of the Holy Spirit in your life? Is there anything that stands in the way? What steps have you taken (or do you need to take) to know the fullness of life in the Spirit of Christ?

Reflective Journaling

Sources

Quotations from the early church fathers are from Brother Kenneth, ed., *From the Fathers to the Churches* (London: William Collins Sons and Co., 1987).

All prayers marked with **JW** are freely adapted from John Wesley, *A Collection of Forms of Prayer for Every Day in the Week*. Library of Methodist Classics. Nashville: United Methodist Publishing House, 1992.

Bowling, John. *Grace-Full Leadership*. Kansas City: Beacon Hill Press of Kansas City, 2011.

Drummond, Henry. *The Greatest Thing in the World*. New York: Grosset and Dunlap, n.d.

Lewis, C. S. *Christian Reflections*. Grand Rapids: Eerdmans, 1967.

———. *Mere Christianity*. London: G. Bles, 1952.

Mann, Edward S. *The Things That Count*. Kansas City: Beacon Hill Press of Kansas City, 1983.

McCartney, Clarence Edward. *The Greatest Texts of the Bible*. Nashville: Abingdon-Cokesbury Press, 1947.

Ratzinger, Joseph. *Jesus of Nazareth*. San Francisco: Ignatius Press, 2011.

———. *On the Way to Jesus Christ*. San Francisco: Ignatius Press, 2005.

Stancliffe, David. *Pilgrim Prayer Book*. London: Continuum, 2003.

Stewart, James S. *The Strong Name*. New York: Charles Scribner's Sons, 1941.

Ten Boom, Corrie. *Clippings from My Notebook*. Thorndike, ME: Thorndike Press, 1983.

Tozer, A. W. *The Knowledge of the Holy*. San Francisco: Harper, 1961.

www.ingramcontent.com/pod-product-compliance
Lightning Source LLC
LaVergne TN
LVHW051519070426
835507LV00023B/3197